BACKSTREET BOYS

30TH ANNIVERSARY CELEBRATION

The Boys in Las Vegas during their *PAPER* magazine interview and photo shoot covering their massive Larger Than Life residency at The AXIS at Planet Hollywood Resort & Casino.

BACKSTREET BOYS 30TH ANNIVERSARY CELEBRATION

KARAH-LEIGH HANCOCK & EMILIA FILOGAMO

FOREWORD BY MELANIE CHISHOLM OF THE SPICE GIRLS

EPIC INK

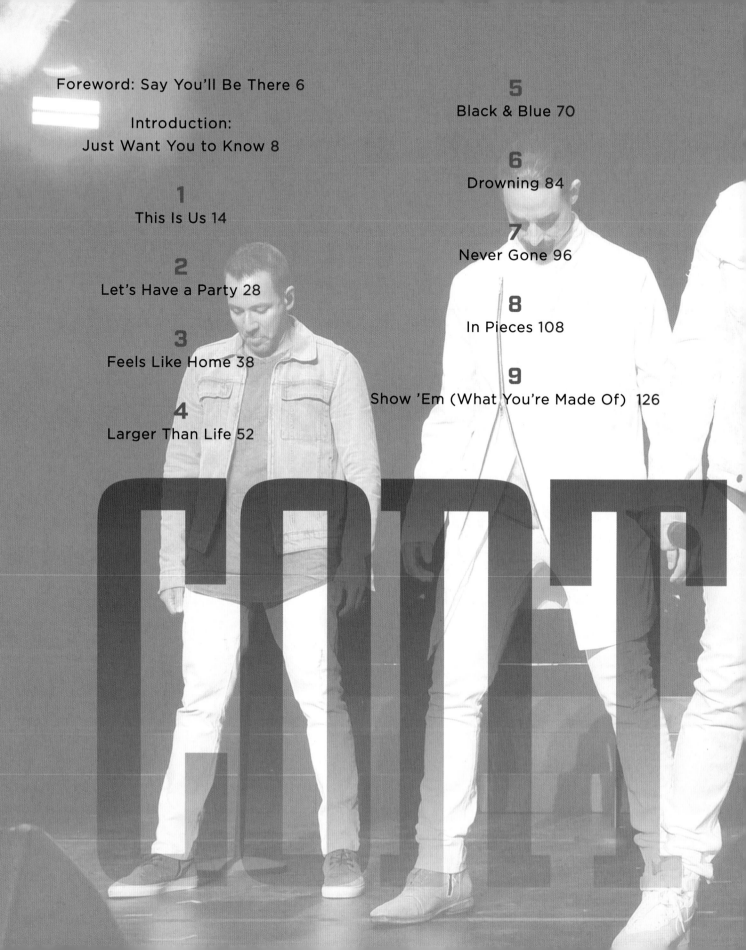

The Backstreet Boys perform at 103.5 KTU's KTUphoria on June 16, 2018, in Jones Beach, New York.

SAY YOU'LL BE THERE

Rewind a quarter of a century to 1998. I'm backstage at the BRIT Awards and the five of us Spice Girls are nervously buzzing about our dressing room, getting ready to perform on television to millions of people. As we all jangle around, winding each other up even more, excitement is starting to bubble out of control. So, we do what we always do in these situations—find a stereo, stick on a CD (it was the '90s, remember!), turn the volume up to ten, and press play.

"Everybody (Backstreet's Back)" is just one of the Backstreet Boys songs that got us girls revved up when we needed it. Anytime I hear Brian's iconic "Everybooodyyyyy," I'm transported straight back to being a Spice Girl during those wild and crazy times. Whenever we got nervous, we'd get the *Backstreet Boys* or *Backstreet's Back* albums on and dance about to get rid of all that nervous energy.

When the Spice Girls started out, there weren't many female pop bands—most were R&B like Eternal, En Vogue, and TLC—so we always looked to the boy bands for inspiration. The UK had Take That and the US had New Kids on the Block—but Backstreet Boys were our favorite. We were fans as soon as we heard "I'll Never Break Your Heart," sometime around Christmas 1995. When the album came out a few months later, we played it over and over—"We Got It Goin' On," "Quit Playin' Games (With My Heart)"... those harmonies! I think it's clear why the band has been so successful; they have great, great songs. On top of that, they were—are still—fantastic vocalists. You cannot knock their abilities. I've always admired their dedication to live performance, as well as their energy and their choreography. Everything was always on point. They were—still are—the true definition of all-rounders. They're flawless.

We first met the boys around the time of their album release, spring 1996. They were already pretty big in Europe at this point, while the Spice Girls were just starting to promote "Wannabe" at radio roadshows around the UK. We were really excited to be out there and doing it, meeting all the other bands and playing for our fans. There's a photo of us from that first meeting, I think it's backstage at a radio show in the north of England. We all look so young and fresh-faced. The boys were incredibly warm and friendly, and we were all excited and energetic—the ten of us immediately got on.

The Spiceys and BSBs ended up being together in Germany a lot throughout 1996 and 1997, as both bands did really well there. We even ended up sharing a dressing room on at least one occasion. Ten popstars in one room—there must have been a lot of noise and a lot of hairspray!

Because the boys were a bit ahead of us at that point, they were really helpful in telling us how things worked, what to expect, what to avoid. Then, when the Spice Girls exploded in 1997 around the same time as their huge second international album, *Backstreet's Back*, we were able to relate to each other even more closely and support each other on this crazy journey. There was a sense of shared experience between us, and it was nice to talk to people who were going through what we were going through.

From 1996 to 2000, we saw the boys at various places around the world. Every time we were in the airport, we had this joke that you could always hear a boy band coming a mile off! They'd all wear these massive shiny puffer jackets that would swish through the airport. We were constantly on and off planes, so if we didn't see each other at an awards show or a TV taping, we'd bump into the boys in departures at Berlin, Barcelona, or Birmingham.

We started out as fans and became peers, which was really lovely. A couple of us Spice Girls have gone onto work with the boys; Emma and Nick both appeared on ABC's talent show *Boy Band* and I opened for them in Dubai in 2018. It was lovely to support them, and I loved watching their show. They're as brilliant live as they are on record.

One of my favorite BSB moments was when my phone started popping off one day in 2018—the boys had dressed up as us during a show and everyone was sending me the pictures. Brian makes a very good Sporty Spice! If I ever need a stand in, I know who to call . . .

It was funny when both bands had "comebacks" a few years ago. Us Spices had a brilliant 2019, when we reformed for a UK and Ireland tour. And it was lovely to see the BSBs come back that same year, stronger than ever, with their new tour and a whole new number-one album, *DNA*, their first since 2000. How brilliant is that?

Our paths have crossed a lot. People often talk about the success of the Spice Girls being down to our individuality, and I think that was part of the magic of the Backstreet Boys too. There were five very distinct personalities that all complimented each other. You've got joker Brian, sensitive and sweet Howie, AJ the rebel (who was a total softie underneath the bad boy charm!), Kevin, who was like our Geri, older and a bit wiser, and then of course Baby Backstreet—aka Nick. Maybe it shouldn't work, but mix us all together and somehow it does.

The other thing that unites us all is that we all went through our personal struggles— and came out the other side. You have this moment of success, which is brilliant, but you do need space to figure out who you are when you're not a Spice Girl or a Backstreet Boy. We were all so young back then— especially Nick and Emma—and we needed some time out to see who we were outside of this pop star bubble. When you're able to come back and really appreciate what you made together, it's not only wonderful for you but it's wonderful for the fans too.

We were inspired by the Backstreet Boys, we had a kinship with them, there was a lot of similarities between the groups, and I think we all really respected each other. It's great to see them back together and killing it harder than ever. Backstreet Boys forever!

Melanie Chisholm
Singer-songwriter, actress, DJ, author, and the one and only Sporty Spice

INTRODUCTION

JUST WANT YOU TO KNOW

The Backstreet Boys perform their a capella song "Breath" in concert on the DNA World Tour on June 28, 2022, in Atlanta, Georgia

TO many people, the Backstreet Boys were simply a boy band—a group of five guys who were put together to make girls scream with delight. They were a group of pretty faces that sparkled plenty of teenage fantasies.

People think they faded away when "bubblegum pop" disappeared around 2003. Some people think the group got back together for the NKOTBSB tour with New Kids on the Block in 2010 or the Las Vegas residency in 2017. Maybe it was the duet with Florida Georgia Line that went to No. 1 on the country charts. Journalists continuously throw around the words "reunion" or "comeback."

Every time the group makes the news for something big, it's always, "Backstreet's Back!" The jokes never get old, but oh, how wrong they are.

What many people do not realize is that the Backstreet Boys, the best-selling boy band in music history, never broke up. They never went away. They didn't disband like other boy bands of the era (we're looking at you, *NSYNC) or break up and get back together (hi, O-Town and New Kids on the Block). They have been going strong since April 20, 1993. Their longest break as a group (2002–2003) didn't even last as long as the COVID-19 pandemic.

AJ, Brian, Kevin, Nick, and Howie have been giving us new music and material for thirty years. While most bands peter out and only tour on old material, the Backstreet Boys are still cranking out No. 1 albums, like their 2019 release, *DNA*. They are still being nominated for Grammy Awards. They are still one of the biggest touring acts, selling out arenas on their 2019 DNA World Tour before it was halted by the pandemic in 2020. Even after the world opened back up a little in 2022, the band sold out venues such as the Hollywood Bowl.

We were already thinking of a project for the Backstreet Boys' thirtieth anniversary when we were approached with the idea for this book. It mixed two of our biggest passions—writing and the Backstreet Boys—so we knew we had to do it. We have hardly been able to contain our excitement among our fellow fans while we worked feverishly on this book because it's that important to us.

The Backstreet Boys are that *important* to us.

To some, the Backstreet Boys really may just be a boy band, but to the Backstreet Army, what they call us fans, they are our world. They are the voices that calm us down when we have panic attacks. They are the melodies we turn to in the best and worst of times. They are the five guys who can put a smile on our faces just by opening their mouths.

This book isn't about telling their full story as a group. That's not our story to tell. It's more about celebrating what they have accomplished in the last thirty years. It's about the fact that they have had it goin' on (pun intended) for thirty years. It's about celebrating what the band has meant to women, men, and all folks, around the world. It's about showcasing their triumphs over the last three decades.

It's about, as Howie likes to say, keeping the Backstreet pride alive.

To me, the Backstreet Boys mean happiness. They came into my life during a time when I needed that. Throughout the years, whenever I needed encouragement, they were there for me, whether it was a lyric, a meeting, or a tweet. If it weren't for Nick Carter, I would not have gone back to college. I would not have become an award-winning journalist. I probably would not have written this book. They are the reason I learned HTML, web, and graphic design. They have introduced me to my love of writing, to my best friends and sisters from another mister, and introduced me to the meaning of life. If it weren't for the Backstreet Boys, I would not be alive today.

People come and go, whether it's family, friends, or acquaintances, but the Backstreet Boys are always there. No other group or performer that I have been a fan of has meant as much to me as the Boys have. It's because of these five guys that I have gotten to experience so much in my life, and just knowing the fact that they know who I am still amazes me. Sometimes it freaks me out a little, but in a good way. I'm proud of the fact that every day I get to help keep the Backstreet pride alive.

The shape of my heart is three letters: B-S-B.

KARAH-LEIGH HANCOCK ★ ATLANTA, GA
KEEPING THE BACKSTREET PRIDE ALIVE SINCE '98

The Backstreet Boys have been a big part of my life since early 1998 when I got their US debut album on cassette tape for my birthday. From that moment, I became more of a fan than before. Their music has always been a constant for me. Dealing with bullying—their music helped me escape that.

Over the years, I began to share news and information on the Boys through various outlets, such as Yahoo Groups and fan forums. Then I started my own fan site for Nick Carter in 2006, called Kaos Online. One would think, why didn't I use Nick's name? Well, I didn't want the same old, same old name. So, instead, I used his nickname, Kaos. I closed the site twelve years later in August 2018. I still maintain the social media accounts for it on Twitter and Instagram, where I continue to post news.

In 2012, I got the opportunity to post news on Nick's official website, thanks to Nick and Eddie Meehan. Can't thank them enough for that opportunity. These days I no longer post on his site, but it was a learning experience that I'll never forget. This was something that I never imagined happening. My fan site was my way of showing support to Nick and the Backstreet Boys and keeping fans informed. If it weren't for BSB or the fans, I don't think the website would have existed as long as it did. There have been moments where I struggled with maintaining the fan site, and that's partly why I closed it in 2018. I knew I couldn't give up being involved with the Backstreet Army, though.

Without them, I wouldn't have met fans from around the world who visited my site frequently. Through social media and because of my website, I've been able to meet many people, and some even in person, all because of the Backstreet Boys. People that I consider friends. While some have come and gone, being a part of the Backstreet Army showed just how amazing people are. The good outweighs the bad.

Do I think I'll ever stop being as involved with fans as I am and being a part of the Backstreet Army? Probably not. While I no longer have a fan site, I help Karah with her site, BSBFangirls.com. I've been a fan for twenty-four years, almost twenty-five. It will be twenty-five prior to their thirtieth anniversary in 2023. They're one of the few artists that I've been a fan of for this long that I don't think I'll stop being a fan.

ABOVE: Emilia Filogamo with Nick Carter during meet and greet at the Nick & Kvnight concert in Pittsburgh, Pennsylvania, on October 1, 2014.

OPPOSITE: Karah-Leigh Hancock poses with the Backstreet Boys in June 2017 at their Larger Than Life Las Vegas residency.

EMILIA FILOGAMO ★ PITTSBURGH, PA
KEEPING THE BACKSTREET PRIDE ALIVE SINCE '98

1
THIS IS US

"I'm expecting big things. They have a lot of natural talent—they dance, they sing, and the pack is well put-together."

—Mark Cheatham, talent agent ★ *Orlando Sentinel*, October 31, 1993

The Backstreet Boys clowning around at a photo shoot in 1995.

COMING TOGETHER

Lou Pearlman, a New York native who was the first cousin of musician Art Garfunkel (of Simon & Garfunkel fame), became captivated with the idea of starting a vocal harmony group, or boy band, after New Kids on the Block chartered one of his planes in the late 1980s. They invited him to a show, where he saw thousands of girls going crazy for them and millions of dollars in sales of albums and merchandise. It was then that he decided to create a similar group.

Pearlman, a businessman who we would later find out also created one of the biggest Ponzi schemes of all time, got his start in the blimp industry, but that wasn't his true calling. After his blimp business crashed, literally and figuratively, he decided to create a boy band of New Kids' caliber. He created a record label, Transcontinental Records, to help make this music dream a reality. Since he knew nothing about show business, Pearlman enlisted the help of veteran Universal Studios singer Gloria Sicoli who had

a long history in the entertainment industry and placed advertisements in the *Orlando Sentinel.* The ads appeared in the newspaper for six days, from July 3 to July 8, 1992. Ads were also placed in the *Florida Blue Sheet,* an entertainment trade publication in the south. They read: "Teen male vocalists: Producer seeks male teen singers that move well between 16–19 years of age. Wanted for New Kids-type singing/dance group. Send photo or bio' of any kind."

"I wanted five guys who could have fun, sound good, and meld perfectly together. It's crucial to get the right mix," Lou told the *Tampa Tribune* in their June 30, 1993, edition.

The Bad Boy

The first to answer the advertisement was Denise, Alexander James McLean's mother. Alex, better known to us today as AJ, was an aspiring performer and auditioned for Pearlman in his living room when he was just fourteen.

During the audition, AJ had to sing one of three New Kids on the Block songs: "I'll Be Loving You Forever," "Didn't I Blow Your Mind," or "Please Don't Go Girl." The song was chosen at random, and he sang to a backing tape. AJ was then asked to dance in any style to the music of his choosing.

Growing up, AJ took dance lessons because of his love of Paula Abdul, where he learned ballet, tap, jazz, hip-hop, and ballroom. He also took fencing lessons. At the age of five, his mother got him into modeling, and he was later featured in JCPenney catalogs. His grandmother also taught him piano and would take him to

RIGHT: An advertisement that was placed by Lou Pearlman in the *Orlando Sentinel* from July 3-8, 1992.

17 ENTERTAINMENT & AUDITIONS

TEEN MALE VOCALIST — Producer seeks male teen singers that move well between 16-19 yrs of age wanted for "New Kids" type singing/dance group. Send photo & bio of any kind (video or audio tape optional) to: TransContinental, 7380 Sand Lake Rd, Suite 200, Orlando, FL 32819. Attn: Gloria Sicoli

Entertainment

Young performer tries out many talents

Though just 14, McLean has lots of experience

By Laurie Whitmore
OF THE SENTINEL STAFF

KISSIMMEE — Like any good performer, Alexander James "A.J." McLean is part chameleon, part philosopher and part child.

At age 14, getting in touch with his inner child isn't a real stretch for McLean.

But don't let the tender age fool you. McLean is a veteran performer with a full resume of stage, film and television credits.

McLean portrays two characters in the Osceola Players' current production of *South Pacific* — Henry the butler and Marcel the assistant to resident huckster Bloody Mary.

The list goes on. McLean is also a professional model, a trained singer, dancer and actor, cartoonist and comic.

Despite his trunk-full of talents, McLean's philosophy is to do one thing and do it well.

"I want to be known for one thing, whatever that is, when I die," said the Denn John Middle School eighth-grader. "The key is to put a lot of love, energy and feeling into whatever you do."

Spotlight
ALEXANDER JAMES MCLEAN

For now, though, McLean is eagerly exploring everything from animation to Shakespeare to Rodgers and Hammerstein.

McLean moved to Central Florida from the West Palm Beach area two years ago. In addition to five years of dance lessons, the bulk of McLean's training came at the Florida Academy of Performing Arts in Boca Raton.

At age 6, McLean started spending nearly every Saturday at the academy, studying the nuts and bolts of the theatrical arts — mime, speech, movement, history, stagecraft.

At age 10, McLean landed the part of Louis in *The King & I* at the Burt Reynolds Dinner Theatre in Jupiter. He was cast in the role even though he had to have his whistling dubbed from backstage during the song, "Give a Little Whistle."

"That play was really great for me, but I couldn't whistle," McLean said. During the show's run, though, McLean's grandparents, Ursula and Adolph Fernandez, taught him to whistle.

McLean's career is definitely a family business. McLean lives in Kissimmee with his mother, Denise, and his whistle-tutors/handlers, the Fernandezes.

The booming film and television industries in Central Florida have been good to McLean, who has landed several roles on Nickelodeon programs and came close to capturing a set of mouse ears as a regular on the new Mickey Mouse Club.

In *South Pacific*, McLean's Central Florida stage debut, McLean has made a good impression on director David Gerrard.

"A.J. is probably the most well-rounded performer in the cast," Gerrard said. "He's terrific to work with."

If McLean has his way, his face will become very familiar to Central Florida audiences — he plans to audition for upcoming musicals from Godspell to The Sound of Music to Into the Woods.

A.J. McLean practices a dance step from 'South Pacific.'

RICHARD SHEPHERD/SENTINEL

LEFT: AJ featured in an article in the May 8, 1992, edition of the *Orlando Sentinel*.

BELOW: AJ during a photo shoot in New York in 1997.

auditions. AJ would go on to perform in twenty-seven school plays, such as *Snow White and the Seven Dwarfs*, *The Nutcracker*, and *Fiddler on the Roof*, to name a few.

When AJ was just eight years old, he landed the role of Little Mike in the 1986 film *Truth or Dare?* In 1991, he played a character named Skunk on the Nickelodeon comedy show *Hi Honey, I'm Home* but he was cut after the pilot episode for being too tall.

Aside from acting, AJ also tried out for the talent competition TV show *Star Search* in 1991 but never received a callback. Around the same time, he also performed at a Latin festival, where he won first place and a thousand-dollar prize. AJ was then hired to perform a forty-five-minute set, showing off his acting, dancing, and singing talents during the sets, as well as his skill as a puppeteer.

"I want to be known for one thing, whatever that is, when I die," AJ told the

Orlando Sentinel in May 1992. "The key is to put a lot of love, energy, and feeling into whatever you do."

AJ became the first Backstreet Boy. With the help of AJ's managers, Jeanne Tanzy Williams and Sybil Hall, Lou Pearlman began organizing the rest of the group.

Part of the school's television class works as a team to get the lights exactly right for filming.   Co-director Boggs explains scene to actors Howard Dorough and Sally Woo...

It's not all glamor and glitz, students find

ABOVE: Photos from an article about Edgewater High School's TV class, featuring Howie, from the *Orlando Centennial*'s November 8, 1990, edition.

RIGHT: The boy formerly known as Tony Donetti becomes Howie D.

The Shy One

At the same time, Tony Donetti, a young singer and actor from Orlando, auditioned. Pearlman and his group of advisers were interested in Tony, but they could not contact him after the audition because they lost his photo and information and were unable to locate his name in the phone book.

Many know him today as Howie D., but prior to auditioning for the Backstreet Boys, Howie had attempted to get into acting under the name Tony Donetti. His manager at the time felt his full name, Howard Dorough, was too formal and gave him the Donetti stage name. As an actor, he landed a few small roles in the movies *Parenthood* and *Cop and a Half*. He would also go on to audition for the Nickelodeon show *Welcome Freshmen*. At fourteen, Howie auditioned for the Latin boy band Menudo, but due to not knowing Spanish, he didn't make the group.

It would be several months before he found out that he had been chosen to join the Backstreet Boys. In a 2015 interview with PopCrush.com, Howie explained how he got a second shot but almost didn't make the group due to his stage name.

"Then I had an agent who asked me to go out for [the same] group, and at the time, I'm like, 'I think I've already done this. I don't want to embarrass myself by going out for this same thing—they must have just not liked me,'" he remembered. "Finally, I said, 'Alright, I'll go for it.' I went to this place, and I got so lost—I was 45 minutes late—that I almost turned around . . . but something told me to go a little bit further."

"I actually found the place and they were like, 'Tony! Oh my God, we lost your picture. We were trying to find a Tony Donetti in the phone book,'" Howie recalled.

Howie then knew he had to change his name. Howard Dorough was still too formal, so he suggested going by Howie D., a name that a friend from his high school choir used to call him. Howie D. became the second member of the Backstreet Boys.

The Baby

Nickolas Gene Carter, originally from New York, lived outside of Tampa in the early '90s. At a young age, Nick had shown interest in music and performing. His mother, Jane, got him voice lessons, and he later also took dance lessons at the Karl and DiMarco School of Theater and Dance. Sandy Karl, co-owner of the Theater and Dance school, was also a choreographer and cheerleader coach for the Tampa Bay Buccaneer cheerleaders. Eventually, Nick began performing with the cheerleaders during the team's halftime shows. Nick spent two years performing at the home games at Houlihan's Stadium. They were called Nick and the Angels.

Nick spent the late 1980s and early 1990s performing at talent shows such as "The New Original Amateur Hour," where he won, and at the Florida State Fair. He also filmed various commercials and had a small, uncredited part as the kid playing on a yellow Slip 'N Slide in the Johnny Depp movie *Edward Scissorhands*.

"The sensitivity and control are unbelievable for such a young age," Nick's vocal coach, Marianne Prinkey, said of his voice in an article in the February 29, 1992, edition of the *Tampa Tribune*.

In October 1992, twelve-year-old Nick auditioned for *The New Mickey Mouse Club*, which would include future performers Britney Spears, Christina Aguilera, and Ryan Gosling, plus two future *NSYNC members JC Chasez and Justin Timberlake. During that time, he also auditioned for the Backstreet Boys. *The New Mickey Mouse Club* offered him a $50,000 contract, while Nick wasn't chosen to be in the Backstreet Boys right away. Though they liked him, he wasn't among their first choices. But when

BELOW LEFT: Nick poses during an early BSB photo shoot.

BELOW RIGHT: A newspaper clipping with a story about a young Nick Carter from the February 29, 1992, edition of the *Tampa Tribune*.

12-year-old Tampa boy hopes to sing, dance way to stardom

By HEATHER REED
Tribune Staff Writer

NORTH TAMPA — In his younger days, Nick Carter used to stand on a tree stump in his back yard and sing to an audience of "blades of grass."

At the ripe old age of 12, Nick hopes to get his big break in show biz today on the "New Original Amateur Hour" hosted by Willard Scott. The show is being taped at Universal Studios in Orlando and will air on the Family Channel at 7:30 p.m. March 22.

Nick, who will sing and dance to Neil Sedaka's "Breaking Up is Hard to Do," is competing against nine others for top honors and a chance for stardom. If he wins, he could be "discovered".

"You see, I'm an actor, too, but I'm mostly interested in singing," the precocious blond said.

Nick auditioned for the amateur hour in January at Evers Casting Connection, but it is far from his first public performance.

He sang the likes of "Runaround Sue" and "God Bless the U.S.A." at the Florida State Fair this year, performed at the MacDill Air Force Base air show last year and took first place for song and dance at the national Show Stoppers contest in North Carolina last year, to name just a few.

Nick, the oldest of five children, attends sixth grade at Orange Grove Elementary School. His parents own and run a retirement home near Forest Hills.

The youngster's career started about three years ago when his mother, Jane, heard him singing "Bridge Over Troubled Water" on the backyard stump and thought she detected something special.

She did, according to Nick's voice coach, Marianne Prinkey.

"The sensitivity and control are unbelievable for such a young man," Prinkey said.

But Nick has more than a good voice, she said. More than anything else, the young man wants to sing, and he puts his heart into his performances.

Tribune photograph by TODD L. CHAPPEL

Nick Carter, 12, hopes to be discovered on television's "New Original Amateur Hour."

"He wants this in the very worst way, and you have to want this in the very worst way if you're going to get it," she said.

Nick's main goal, his mother said, is to get a recording contract.

To that end, he has a personal manager and attends

See KID, Page 2

another boy quit within a week, Lou, Jeanne Tanzy Williams, and Sybil Hall looked at the footage of Nick's audition again and asked him to join.

Nick had to choose between a guaranteed $50,000 contract or the Backstreet Boys. He chose the Backstreet Boys.

AJ, Howie, and Nick joined an original lineup that also included performers Sam Licata and Burk Parsons. They all met for the first time during AJ's birthday on January 9, 1993. According to Denise McLean's 2003 book *Backstreet Mom*, there was also an alternate member named Damon who eventually left the band because he found out he would not be performing on stage.

The group became the Backstreet Boys, named after the new Backstreet Market shopping center that had recently opened in Orlando. The spot had become a hangout of sorts for local teenagers and those vacationing in the popular International Drive area of Orlando near Universal Studios.

The Big Brother

Before the group could make a name for itself, there were already issues arising, according to Denise's book. Burk eventually left the group, and another young man named Charles Edward joined. But Charles didn't last long, and then one day before a performance, Sam decided the group could not use one of his songs, and he left the group too.

But a promising young man from Kentucky was in the audience that night, and Lou already knew him.

Kevin Scott Richardson, originally from Lexington, KY, spent most of his early years on a ten-acre farm and singing in a church choir. In 1981, after his family moved to Estill County, KY, he taught himself to play the piano at a summer camp his father managed.

After graduating from high school, Kevin was torn between joining the Air Force (to join the Air Force band) and attending the New York American Music and Dramatic

RIGHT: After working at Walt Disney World as a dance instructor, among other entertainment jobs, Kevin joined the Backstreet Boys.

Having first seen BSB in a high school auditorium, Deana visits the group during the opening run of their Las Vegas residency in 2017.

BACKSTREET ARMY, ASSEMBLE!

My love for the Backstreet Boys started in 1995 when they performed at my brother's high school in Baltimore, MD. I remember seeing their choreographed dance moves and hearing their a cappella angelic voices that literally gave me goosebumps! They gave out a demo tape that I played so much you would think the tape would snap. After graduating, my brother joined the US Coast Guard and was sent overseas to Germany. I remember a call when he said, "That group from my high school is huge here," and that he was going to mail me some merch. Every week I would receive a package with VHS tapes, magazines, and T-shirts. My addiction started at the age of eleven. Flash forward to the present day, seeing these "boys" over eighty times around the US with countless meet and greets, being featured in their Grammy Museum exhibit, and even joining them on their 2018 cruise. Backstreet Boys hold such a special place in my heart, and I have met so many longtime friends over our bond with these men. I will forever be a fan and forever be grateful for the joy they bring to my life. Here's to thirty more years, boys!

DEANA A. ★ BALTIMORE, MD
KEEPING THE BACKSTREET PRIDE ALIVE SINCE '95

Academy. But then something pointed him to Florida. His parents had just gone on a cruise to the Bahamas, where they saw many young entertainers. They reminded Kevin's mom, Ann, of him, and she suggested he audition for an entertaining job on one of the cruise lines. In the end, Kevin decided to go to Orlando, FL, instead, where he got a job at Walt Disney World in 1990.

While he worked at Walt Disney World, he was an MGM Studios tour guide and a cast member. He would perform as Aladdin, Leonardo of the Teenage Mutant Ninja Turtles, Prince Eric, and others. At night, Kevin did dinner theater, performing as an Italian gangster in a musical review, where he sang songs from *Chicago*, *Cabaret*, and more.

But Kevin's stay in Orlando wasn't long. He headed back home in June 1991 after receiving a call that his father Jerald's colon cancer had gotten worse. His father ultimately passed away on August 26, 1991. Kevin stayed in Kentucky for almost a year afterward and got a job, but his mother encouraged him to return to Orlando. Back in Orlando in 1992, he returned to work at Disney World, modeled, and taught ballroom dancing (as he was a certified Latin and ballroom instructor). He was also an extra in the movie *My Girl*.

At the time, Kevin's then-girlfriend's roommate's boyfriend (yes, a tongue twister) worked for Lou Pearlman. Bob Dunham knew about Kevin's dreams of becoming a pop or rock star and told Lou about the tall Kentucky boy. As fate would have it, Kevin then met a woman at a convention who happened to be the wife of Bob Fischetti, Lou Pearlman's closest business associate. In March 1993, Kevin Richardson became a Backstreet Boy.

"When Kevin sang with the other boys, it was clear that he was just what we had been looking for," Denise McLean wrote in her book.

This left the group with just one spot remaining. Kevin knew exactly who to call—his cousin, Brian Littrell.

The Boy Next Door

At the age of seven, Brian sang his first solo at the Porter Memorial Baptist Church in Lexington, KY. He sang in the choir and was voted President of the Youth Chorus. His choir teacher, Barry Turner, suggested he could make money with his singing voice, so he performed at weddings. He was also in his high school's production of *Grease*.

RIGHT: A fateful phone call brought Brian, pictured during an early photoshoot, to Orlando, to complete the band's sound.

Brian aspired to become a professional basketball player, but due to his five-foot-seven height, he struggled. He changed tracks and decided he wanted to be a music minister.

As the story is told, Brian received a message while sitting in his high school history class on April 19, 1993. He had a phone call from his cousin, Kevin, who had been living in Orlando. Kevin told him about the group he was in and how they had one more space open; Brian would be perfect for it.

After talking with his parents that evening and auditioning by phone that night, Brian was on the next flight to Orlando to meet AJ, Nick, and Howie for the first time. The group of five performed together for the first time that day, and the Backstreet Boys sound was complete.

THE EARLY DAYS

The Backstreet Boys' first performance as a group came on May 8, 1993, at Orlando's Sea World in front of three thousand students. The audience went crazy for the group. While they only performed four songs, just hearing the crowd scream for the five boys made them want to achieve more. They spent five days a week rehearsing in a warehouse/blimp hanger with no air conditioner that Lou had rented.

Two months after their first performance, Johnny and Donna Wright were hired as managers. Johnny had previously worked as the road manager for New Kids on the Block. After hiring the Wrights, the Backstreet Boys soon began touring across the South and along the East Coast at schools, restaurants, malls—anywhere they could. They would also perform at a few clubs, though some of them were underage and had to leave right after the gig. They also got the chance to perform at the Second Annual Ronald McDonald Children's Charities of South Florida in Fort Lauderdale in June 1993, a high-profile gala that honored Whitney Houston.

ABOVE: A front-page story about the Backstreet Boys performing at a Dayton, Ohio, high school from the *Dayton Daily News'* September 27, 1995, edition.

BELOW: An advertisement to meet the Backstreet Boys at Bealls in the *Tampa Tribune* on August 26, 1994.

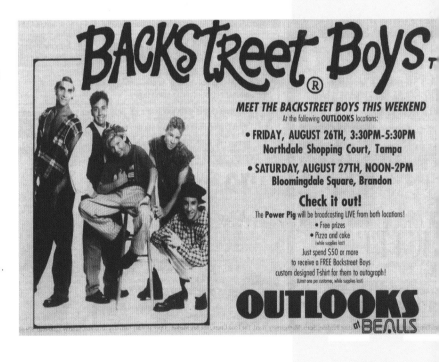

The Backstreet Boys' first concert with all five members was held at Grad Nite at Sea World on May 6, 1993, in Orlando, Florida. There were around three thousand high school seniors in attendance, and they went crazy for the Boys.

"There are no sustainers out there," Johnny Wright told the *Orlando Sentinel* in the October 31, 1993, edition. "Vanilla Ice came and went, M.C. Hammer came and went, but the Beach Boys are still selling out arenas. That's what we would like to do with the Backstreet Boys. We're not in it for the short term; we're in for a long time."

From August to November 1993, the Backstreet Boys embarked on a ten-

week tour of high schools across the United States. They were ambassadors for Students Against Destructive Decisions (SADD). But it wasn't all good times.

"We were somewhere on the East Coast, we were in this auditorium, and we're doing our stuff, and the entire sound system went out," AJ recounted on an episode of *The Kelly Clarkson Show* in 2022. "No mics, no nothing. So, Brian is basically trying to get

RIGHT: The Boys, circa 1996.

OPPOSITE: When they're this cute, is it any wonder the world fell in love? (The Boys, circa 1996.)

everybody to calm down and stop yelling and screaming. They got really quiet, and we just sang straight a cappella, and we won them over."

JIVE TALKIN'

Jive Records was not the first record label to show an interest in the Backstreet Boys. In 1993, Mercury Records had almost signed the group but unfortunately didn't. According to Tyler Gray's 2008 book, *The Hit Charade*, singer John Cougar Mellencamp had threatened to leave the label if they got into the boy band

business. So, Mercury Records didn't pick up the option on the Backstreet Boys—but it wouldn't be long before they had another deal.

In February 1994, the Backstreet Boys gained the interest of Jive Records. David McPherson had worked at Mercury Records when the group was in discussions with the label but had since gone to work at Jive as an A&R director. According to an industry profile on David Renzer, then senior vice president/general manager of Zomba Music Publishing, he and Jeff Fenster, then senior vice president/A&R at Zomba/Jive Records, flew out to Cleveland, Ohio, to watch the Backstreet Boys perform at a local high

BELOW: The Boys perform in Germany in 1996.

LEFT: "I saw five guys who looked like they were stars," said David McPherson, the man who signed the Boys to Jive Records. The Boys are pictured here around 1995.

school during a Mothers Against Drunk Driving event.

David McPherson would end up being the man to sign the Backstreet Boys to Jive Records, with David Renzer also working on the deal.

"Everybody thought I was crazy," McPerson told the *St. Louis Post-Dispatch* in their February 17, 2000, edition. "At the time, it was a weird thing for me to do. I saw five guys who looked like they were stars. They had great voices for a pop group. You don't hear a lot of pop groups who can sing for real. They were tight, well-groomed, well-developed. And I felt like, hey, there are always gonna be young kids who'll put five good-looking boys up on their wall."

At the time, Jive Records' clients were mainly hip-hop and R&B artists, such as A Tribe Called Quest and Aaliyah. In the late 1990s, after signing the Backstreet Boys, Jive would go on to sign other pop acts like Britney Spears and *NSYNC.

2

LET'S HAVE A PARTY

"The show included a mixture of their trademark a cappella harmonizing, along with several pop songs done to booming prerecorded music. They danced energetically and sang to the students and history teacher, evoking screams of delight from the 350-member, mostly freshman audience."

—Katherine Ulimer ★ *Dayton Daily News*, September 27, 1995

What's a boy band without their matching outfits? The Backstreet Boys photographed in 1995.

FIRST TASTE OF SUCCESS

ABOVE: A clipping from "The Rave" classifieds from the February 10, 1995, edition of the *Orlando Sentinel*, with a fan asking when they can buy a Backstreet Boys CD.

BELOW: The Boys, photographed in Stuttgart in November 1997, open mail from adoring fans.

After Jive Records signed the Backstreet Boys in 1994, the label sent the group to Sweden to work with some producers at Cheiron Studios in Stockholm. The producers there—Denniz PoP, Herbert Crichlow, and Max Martin—had had some success with Ace of Base ("The Sign" and "All That She Wants") and Robyn ("Show Me Love").

Denniz PoP began his career in music as a DJ in the mid-1980s and began creating mixes of hit songs for nightclubs. This led to Denniz working on several successful songs in Europe before he received a demo from a Swedish group named Ace of Base. He started working with Ace of Base, and after

their success, Denniz created Cheiron with Tom Taloma.

Max Martin's music career began with him in a glam heavy metal band called It's Alive in the mid-1980s. The band eventually landed a record deal with Denniz PoP's Cheiron Records, and after It's Alive disbanded, Denniz hired Max at Cheiron.

The Backstreet Boys put their careers in the hands of these producers, and it was a good decision. One of the songs written and recorded during the first sessions was "We've Got It Goin' On," which ended up being the group's first single. The song was written by Max, Denniz, and songwriter Herbert Crichlow. "We've Got It Goin' On"

The music video for "We've Got It Goin' On" was filmed in Orlando, FL, on August 19, 1995. The high temperature that day was ninety-three degrees, and the Boys were shooting outside wearing leather and jeans! Talk about hot!

was released to radio across Europe and the United States in August 1995. The Boys promoted the single not only in the United States but also in Europe, holding a launch party at Planet Hollywood in London and making their first television appearances in Europe.

"Here's a tip: Watch out for the Backstreet Boys, a great new group from Orlando. Their single, 'We've Got It Goin' On,' hits stores on Monday, and it's going to take the hearts of females everywhere by storm," teenage reporter Seasen Acevedo said in the September 13, 1995, edition of the *Miami Herald*.

While the single only climbed to No. 69 in the US on the *Billboard* Hot 100, it was a Top 5 hit in Germany (No. 4), Belgium (No. 5), Austria (No. 3), France (No. 5), the Netherlands (No. 5), Switzerland (No. 3), Scotland (No. 3), and the United Kingdom (No. 3). It was a Top 20 hit in Finland, Iceland, Ireland, and Sweden.

After constant promotion, such as performing halftime a cappella shows at basketball games, the Boys were invited to join the Smash Hits Road Show Tour in December 1995, replacing EYC. Artists such as Sean Maguire, Deuce, and Boyzone were also on the tour. The Boys were also added to PJ and Duncan's Christmas Cracker show, replacing EYC again, traveling the United Kingdom and playing

in such venues as the Royal Albert Hall in London.

The hard work was paying off.

"I discovered the Backstreet Boys in late 1995," Audrey Tisserand, a French fan, said. "I first heard them on French radio with 'We've Got It Goin' On.' I can even

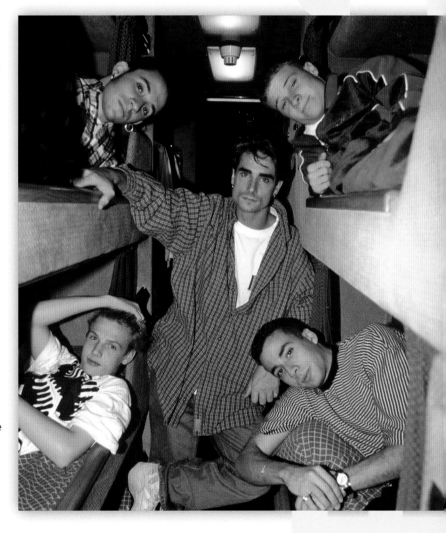

BELOW: The Boys in Birmingham, England, in 1995.

ABOVE: The Boys in Orlando in 1996, where it all began.

"Florida's fresh-faced four-piece new boy band pop sensation—and they will be massive," music reviewer Simon Wilson of the *Evening Post* in Nottingham, England, said in the December 15, 1995, edition of the paper. (Note that Wilson forgot one of the Boys in the *five*-piece group—I wonder who he left out?) "Slick harmonies around a well-crafted pop ballad and looks that the kids will die for—or whatever it is they do. (8/10)."

The ballad would go on to be released later in 1996 to other markets but ended up being a solid Top 10 hit in Australia (No. 10), Austria (No. 5), Belgium (No. 4), Europe (No. 6), Germany (No. 5), the Netherlands (No. 3), Sweden (No. 7), Switzerland (No. 2), and the UK (No. 8).

OH, CANADA!

While heading out on their first headlining tour, the We Wanna Be With You Tour, promoting and working on their first album, the Backstreet Boys were making a little noise in Canada—mainly Quebec to begin with—thanks to some DJs from Montreal that had heard them in Europe. When the Boys went to Montreal, they caused a mob at a mall while doing promotion. A few months later, more than sixty thousand people came to see their concert at a hot-air balloon festival in St. Jean sur Richelieu, and they had a sold-out concert a month later.

remember what the DJ said to introduce them—'and now a new group coming from the USA with their song "We've Got It Goin' On." Remember their name: the Backstreet Boys.' They got me hooked on the first notes."

The Boys ended up winning Best New Tour Act at the 1995 Smash Hits Awards in the United Kingdom. They also received their first gold records when "We've Got It Goin' On" went gold in Germany and Austria. Before 1995 was over, the Boys released their second single in the UK and Europe, "I'll Never Break Your Heart."

Backstreet Boys sold ten million copies internationally in thirty countries before their US self-titled debut was ever released.

LEFT: Hilde Schrøder poses with the Backstreet Boys during the DNA World Tour in 2019. Howie holds a photo of Hilde before she lost weight. The photo is shown below. ABOVE: The Boys perform on ABC's *Good Morning America* in the summer of 2018.

BACKSTREET ARMY, ASSEMBLE!

I've always been a fangirl, but when Backstreet Boys started, and I saw them on TV for the first time, I knew that the Boys would change my life. This was in February 1996. They had two songs out, and I had them on repeat. My friends and I traveled to Germany to maybe meet them, and we did. Since that day, I've been a part of the BSB Army. When I lost my mother in 2005, the Backstreet Boys were a big part of me holding it together. She died a few weeks before the Boys came to Oslo. I don't remember that much from the concert, but when I met Howie that night, he could see that something was wrong. I told him what had happened, and I got a big hug. Then, three years later, he asked me how I was. I know they care about us fans.

HILDE SCHRØDER ★ OSLO, NORWAY
KEEPING THE BACKSTREET PRIDE ALIVE SINCE '96

ABOVE and OPPOSITE: The Backstreet Boys pose for photos while out and about in Oslo, Norway, at various times in 1996.

"Even more eye-popping, all of this was achieved without benefit of an actual album," Mark Lepage said in the September 18, 1996, edition of the (Montreal) *Gazette*. "Maybe it was Howie's falsetto, or Brian's cheekbones, or Nick's blondeness, or Kevin's understated machismo; maybe AJ's energy was to blame."

Once the Boys had a following in Quebec, fans from other parts of Canada heard about them. That was when two fans told YTV's *The Hit List* host Tarzan Dan about the boy band.

"Montreal had already picked up on what was going on in Europe. So, they were playing them on the radio, and they did a concert in Montreal, and the record label flew us to Montreal to interview them because they knew it was going to be huge," Tarzan Dan told the "You Me and YTV" YouTube channel in an interview.

The Boys traveled to Toronto to film *The Hit List* the next day, where Nick, AJ, Brian, Kevin, and Howie surprised the two fans on

the television show. Tarzan Dan would end up being the first person to help the Boys break into English-speaking parts of Canada.

"My earliest memory of Backstreet Boys wasn't actually an album. It was the *Backstreet Boys: Live in Concert* VHS from Germany," Gemma, a Backstreet Boys fan from Mississauga, Ontario, Canada, said. "I was a huge fan of the Spice Girls during the time I got into Backstreet Boys, and I think this was a gift because my parents saw me watching both groups on the Canadian music video countdown show YTV's *The Hit List*."

THE FIRST BACKSTREET BOYS ALBUM

In late April 1996, the Boys released their third single, "Get Down (You're the One For Me)." The song was another Top 10 hit in most countries, even hitting No. 1 in

Lithuania and No. 2 in Canada. The music video, which features the band dancing inside a disco ball with other people dancing around inside the ball, ended up winning the group their first MTV Europe Video Music Award. That same year, the MTV Select Award was introduced, a new award where viewers voted for their favorites in a nine-hour marathon. The Backstreet Boys were nominated against Boyzone, Jamiroquai, Oasis, and the Spice Girls and became the first to win.

With three singles already released, the Backstreet Boys' first self-titled album was finally released on May 6, 1996, in Europe.

"It combines perfect pop with heavenly harmonies and showcases the great vocal versatility which the five band members possess," Jim Lawn said in the October 18, 1996, edition of the *Lennox Herald* (Scotland).

Backstreet Boys would be released later in the United Kingdom (September) and Canada (October). It was a No. 1 album in Austria, Canada, Germany, Hungary, Malaysia, and Switzerland, and the group received its first platinum album award from Germany. The album eventually went platinum in eleven other countries.

According to a December 9, 1996, article in the *Ottawa Citizen*, Quebec accounted for over half of all Canadian sales of the Backstreet Boys' debut album. "We're huge in Montreal. Exactly why, I'm not sure," Richardson said in the same article. "Basically, girls seem to love us."

The Boys started their second headlining tour, Backstreet Boys: Live in Concert, in November 1996 and sold out all European dates. The thirty-two Canadian dates sold out in twenty minutes, so more shows were added in March of the following year.

Along with the release of their first album, three hit singles, and countless sold-out shows, the group was also racking up awards across Europe, including Gold

LEFT: Marisol Arroyo talks with AJ McLean. ABOVE: AJ showing off his great sense of style. Just one of the reasons why he is Marisol's favorite Backstreet Boy.

BACKSTREET ARMY, ASSEMBLE!

As a fan since the beginning (and I will be till the end of time!), I've experienced nothing but the best with the Boys and have met the most incredible people that I could ever meet and gotten to know in their fans.

One amazing time was when a bunch of us fans got together and went to *TRL* to protest MTV not playing enough Backstreet Boys with new music being out. Brian called me to let the fans know he was watching live and thanked us from the bottom of his heart for the love and support. While I and some of the fans I've met along the way might not have as much time to hang out now because we're mommies, no matter what, I thank them for all they have done to support Backstreet.

Meeting AJ too was like all my dreams had come true! I was finally able to meet someone who I admired as a singer, writer, poet, and amazing human. Over the years, I have made the greatest memories and gotten the most amazing photos/videos of shows and meeting encounters. Unfortunately, I lost them all to Hurricane Sandy, so now I just have all these memories and events as mental notes. I want to thank the Backstreet Boys for being who they are, being something to listen to when needed, or just to annoy someone else's ear off (hehe).

MARISOL ARROYO ★ PLAINVIEW, NY
KEEPING THE BACKSTREET PRIDE ALIVE SINCE '95

Pop Group from the Bravo Otto Awards in Germany.

"If I was a 13-year-old girl, I'd look forward to getting dressed for school," an album review said in the September 13, 1996, edition of the *Evening Post* in Nottingham, England. "And I'd probably love this album. Great pop music by God-fearing Americans. (8/10)."

A fourth single, "Quit Playing Games (With My Heart)," another Max Martin and Herbie Crichlow song destined to be a hit, was released in October 1996. The song was their biggest hit to date, going No. 1 in Austria, Czech Republic, Europe, Germany, Lithuania, and Switzerland, and

No. 2 in the UK. The single went platinum in Germany and gold in Australia, Austria, and Poland.

The Boys had begun working on their sophomore album in the fall of 1996 and continued to promote their first album well into 1997. The fifth and final single from their debut album was released—"Anywhere For You." The song was co-written by "I Swear" songwriter Gary Baker and didn't fire up the charts like its predecessor. "Anywhere For You" only went number one in Lithuania and was a Top 5 hit in Denmark (No. 3), the Netherlands (No. 5), Switzerland (No. 3), and the UK (No. 4).

Now it was time to go home.

LEFT: The Boys in Munich, Germany, in 1996.

3
FEELS LIKE HOME

"Most surprising was the quality of the band members' voices . . . Unlike, say, the New Kids on the Block or their female equivalent, the Spice Girls, these Boys really can sing."

—Shawn Ohler ★ *The Edmonton Journal*, April 3, 1997

The Boys taking a break during the filming of the music video for their song, "As Long as You Love Me."

GIRLS IN THE USA

Just like the weather, popular music can change. When the Backstreet Boys released "We've Got It Goin' On" in the United States in 1995, grunge and rap were the most popular music genres on mainstream radio. But something was changing, and that change was that pop music was about to hit its next big wave.

Due to the Backstreet Boys' popularity in Canada, fans just across the border in the States were learning about the group. Disc jockeys across the US had begun playing "Quit Playing Games (With My Heart)" before the song was released in America, especially in areas such as New York, Detroit, and Chicago. Seeing the success of groups such as the Spice Girls, who had their first big hit, "Wannabe," in early 1997, and songs like Hanson's "MMMBop," Jive Records knew it was time to market the Backstreet Boys in the United States.

"Quit Playing Games (With My Heart)" almost wasn't the first single. Jive Records wanted to release Mutt Lange's "If You Want It To Be Good Girl (Get Yourself A Bad Boy)." Mutt Lange, who was Shania Twain's husband at the time, was a hitmaker. But the Boys said no because they hated the song. Jive reluctantly agreed. The Boys also wanted to reshoot the very cheesy music video for "Quit Playing Games (With My Heart)"—they call it the "beefcake" video—

BELOW: Backstreet Boys holding an award for Group Album of the Year at the Billboard Music Awards on December 7, 1998, in Las Vegas, Nevada.

but Jive wanted to focus more on radio than television.

"Quit Playing Games (With My Heart)" was officially released to radio in the United States in April 1997 and debuted at No. 24 on the June 28, 1997, *Billboard* Hot 100 chart. It would go on to stay on the chart for a whopping forty-three weeks and peaked at No. 2 on September 7, 1997, without the help of MTV.

With the success of "Quit Playing Games (With My Heart)," Jive Records began a huge campaign to put the Backstreet Boys in front of audiences beyond radio and television. Working with teen magazines such as *Tiger Beat*, *Bop*, *16*, and *Teen Machine*, Jive also began putting sampler cassettes in Kaboodle make-up cases that were sold at J.C. Penney department stores. They also sent out sampler cassettes to cheerleader camps, and the Backstreet Boys began performing a concert series at Walmart stores across the country.

On *Billboard*'s *Pop Shop Podcast* in July 2022, Kevin reminisced about when he heard the song on the radio for the first time. "I remember my mom was visiting me in Orlando, FL, and we had gone shopping and to dinner, and it came on the radio," he said. "We were in the parking lot, and we were getting back in our car, and I started the car. It was on the radio. We opened the doors, and we got out and danced in a parking lot. That's an amazing memory for me."

For Rachael Jessie from Kentucky, she remembers the first time she heard "Quit Playing Games (With My Heart)" on the radio.

"I was hooked right away!" Rachael said. "So on a trip to the mall, I bought the album *Backstreet Boys*. Oh gosh, loved it so! First

ABOVE: The Backstreet Boys in Cologne, Germany, in March 1998.

time I saw them on TV was MTV's *Spring Break '98*. From there on, I had to see everything they were on and tape it!"

BACKSTREET'S BACK?

The Backstreet Boys had been working on their sophomore international release when it was finally time to release an album in the United States. While the rest of the world received *Backstreet's Back* on August 11, 1997, the States received the second version of *Backstreet Boys* on August 12, 1997. This time, the album included six songs that were on the first international *Backstreet Boys* album and five songs from *Backstreet's Back*.

The Backstreet Boys held a press conference and live concert at the Virgin

Megastore in Times Square to celebrate the release of the second edition of *Backstreet Boys*, and it was packed. The event was also simulcast in thirty countries and on the Internet. In Montreal alone, over two thousand fans turned up at the Spectrum, a music venue, to watch the televised event, with some fans camping out overnight.

In the United States, the new version of *Backstreet Boys* debuted at No. 29 on the *Billboard* 200 chart the week of August 30, 1997, with only forty thousand copies sold. Five months later, it peaked at No. 4 on the January 31, 1998, chart. The album ended up spending 133 weeks on the *Billboard* 200 charts in the US and selling fourteen million copies. On *Billboard*'s Year-End chart, the album charted at No. 140 in 1997, but on the 1998 chart, it landed at No. 4.

The first single from the album internationally was the Denniz PoP/Max Martin up-tempo "Everybody (Backstreet's Back)." The single ended up being a No. 1 hit in Hungary, Romania, and Spain and a Top 5 hit in twenty-one other countries. However, the song was not included in the first editions of the US debut.

Once the group noticed that the new single was being picked up by Canadian radio stations and stations along the border in New York and Detroit, the guys went to Jive. They asked to have the song added to their US debut album. Jive Records

president Barry Weiss thought it would be strange to have a song called "Backstreet's Back" on a debut album.

Eventually, the song was added, and the album was re-released in early 1998. Although, this version of the song differed from the original on *Backstreet's Back*. It was an extended version of the song with a music break in the middle, replacing Nick's bridge from the original recording.

One of the last songs to be included on both albums ended up being the second single on both. "As Long As You Love Me," another Max Martin-penned pop song, marked the first time the band had the same song out as a single in every country at the same time.

While the song went No. 1 in Lithuania, New Zealand, Romania, and the UK and was a Top 5 hit in seventeen other countries, it didn't crack the *Billboard* Hot 100 in the US since it wasn't released as a commercial single to purchase. It did peak at No. 4 on the *Billboard* Hot 100 Airplay chart, spending a total of fifty-six weeks on the chart, and went to No. 3 on the US Adult Contemporary and US Mainstream Top 40 radio charts. Unlike "Quit Playing Games (With My Heart)," the music video became a staple on MTV and VH1.

The group began making appearances on US television shows like *The View*, *Live with Regis and Kathy Lee*, *The Ricki Lake Show*, and *Saturday Night Live*, and they even

> **Billboard released a Greatest of All Time chart in 2015, and on their Billboard 200 album chart, Backstreet Boys' debut US album, Backstreet Boys, charted at No. 42.**

OPPOSITE: The Boys during the 1998 MTV Video Music Awards at the Universal Amphitheatre in Universal City, California.

hosted ABC's "TGIF" Friday night lineup. At the same time, they were appearing on top television shows across the world, like the UK's *Top of the Pops*, Germany's *Interaktiv*, and Italy's *Roxy Bar*, and were all over Canada's Musique Plus channel.

The Backstreet Boys were *everywhere*.

EVERYBODY

When "Everybody (Backstreet's Back)" was released as the third single in the US, it debuted at No. 24 on the *Billboard* Hot 100 on April 14, 1998. It was the highest-ranking debut that week. The song managed to peak at No. 4 on May 19, 1998, and stayed on the chart for twenty-two weeks.

Each guy had their own character for the video: Brian was a werewolf, Nick a mummy, Howie a vampire, AJ the Phantom of the Opera, and Kevin was Dr. Jekyll and Mr. Hyde. The video was filmed on the same set as the movie *Casper*.

"The whole thing was this giant, stressful, immensely-dangerous shoot for me," video director Joseph Kahn told Billboard.com in 2017. "Trying to do something on that scale, doing all the editing and everything myself, racing against time because they were on a

The first version of "Quit Playing Games (With My Heart)" that was released in Europe only had Brian Littrell singing lead vocals. Once Nick Carter's voice changed during puberty, Jive Records flew Max Martin to London to record Nick's vocals, which would end up becoming the final version of the song.

flight the next morning, and trying to keep control of the money."

In the end, MTV loved the video, and it was put in rotation on the network.

Besides reaching No. 4 on the *Billboard* Hot 100 chart, the song also peaked at No. 11 on the US Mainstream Top 40 and No. 14 on the US Rhythmic charts.

HELLO, MTV!

Around that same time, MTV launched a new Top 10 countdown show called *Total Request*. The show aired weeknights on the network and was hosted by Carson Daly. Fans could send in requests for their favorite music videos, and those with the most requests would air on the countdown. "Everybody (Backstreet's Back)" was one of the videos to be featured on the countdown and reached No. 1 multiple times.

That same year the guys got their first ever MTV Video Music Award nominations for Best Group Video and Best Dance Video for the "Everybody" video. They won Best Group Video and performed the song on the live award show.

MTV merged two of its programs, *MTV Live* and *Total Request,* to form *Total Request Live*, which premiered on September 14, 1998. *Total Request Live*, better known as *TRL*, would become a staple for the Backstreet Boys and their fans to request their music on. When you got home from school or between classes, you watched *TRL*. While the groups' videos had appeared on *Total Request*, *TRL* was the show where fans could catch world premieres of the newest music videos and

Mara Sansolo poses with the Backstreet Boys in Las Vegas at Caesars Palace in April 2022.

BACKSTREET ARMY, ASSEMBLE!

I became a fan in 1997, when I was in the fourth grade. I grew up in the Tampa area, and I was keenly aware of my proximity to the Boys. I spent a lot of time at the mall with my mom. We would be sitting at the food court, having a pretzel, and any time a group of teenage boys would pass us, she would say, "Look! It's the Backstreet Boys!" and darn if it didn't turn my head every time. What if that was truly the time that they all came to my mall? My mom passed away in 1999, and those memories have stuck with me ever since. It is one of the few things that I remember laughing about and enjoying after she got sick.

MARA SANSOLO ★ COLUMBIA, SC
KEEPING THE BACKSTREET PRIDE ALIVE SINCE '97

appearances whenever the Backstreet Boys were there to promote new albums.

The first Backstreet Boys music video to chart on the show was "I'll Never Break Your Heart" on September 19, 1998, at No. 1. It was on the countdown for forty-four days and reached No. 1 fourteen times. The song peaked on the *Billboard* Hot 100 charts at No. 35 and on the US Mainstream Top 40 at No. 4 but solidified the group's popularity on the Adult Contemporary chart. "I'll Never Break Your Heart" gave the group their first No. 1 song in the United States.

The final single from both the international *Backstreet's Back* and the Boys' US debut album was "All I Have to Give." The single was released on January 14, 1998, internationally and was released to US audiences on November 24 that same year. It was the first song to feature lead vocals by all five members. "All I Have to Give" was a No. 1 hit in Hungary, Spain, and the United Kingdom and was a No. 5 hit in seven countries, including on the US *Billboard* Hot 100. The song was another hit for the group, reaching No. 8 on Adult Contemporary, No. 30 on Adult Top 40, and No. 7 on Mainstream Top 40. On the Hot 100, it landed at No. 5.

The video's debut on the *TRL* countdown came on November 17 at No. 2. It would stay on the countdown for sixty-five days before retiring on March 3, 1999. It landed at the No. 1 spot thirty-two times.

HOMECOMING

The Backstreet Boys organized a charity concert on March 15, 1998, outside the

RIGHT and OPPOSITE: Photos of the Boys during the making of the *Millennium* album in Sweden in 1998.

Hard Rock Cafe at Universal Studios Florida in Orlando. The event, "Orlando Bands Together," was set to help victims of tornados that had hit Central Florida earlier that year. Money raised during the event would be donated to the *Orlando Sentinel*/CFN13 Tornado Relief Fund and the Red Cross Relief Fund. *NSYNC, LFO, and C&C Factory were among those set to perform. Over ten thousand people attended.

Later that year, on October 7, 1998, the Backstreet Boys were presented with keys to the city of Orlando by Mayor Glenda E. Hood for raising $250,000 during the benefit concert. Three thousand fans were in attendance to watch the Boys receive keys to the city and perform a little a cappella. October 7 was also declared Backstreet Boys Day in Orlando. Fans all around the world continue to celebrate Backstreet Boys Day to this day.

On December 31, 1998, the Backstreet Boys performed to a sold-out crowd in their hometown at the Orlando Arena for a New Year's Eve concert. The concert, titled "Backstreet Boys: Coming Home," would air on Pay-Per-View on February 6, 1999, then on Fox Family (now known as Freeform) in July 1999. It was also released on VHS/DVD as *Homecoming: Live in Orlando*. This would be the first concert event the group filmed in the US. The pay-per-view airing reached 160,000 views, making it the first event to reach 100,000 views for a pay-per-view event. The VHS was certified triple platinum by RIAA for sales of 300,000 on December 23, 1999.

The concert featured the guys singing songs from their US debut, as well as songs

from their two international albums. The setlist also included five solo performances from the guys, such as "Nobody But You," a song performed by Kevin on their international debut, and "That's What She Said," sung by Brian on *Backstreet's Back*. Nick sang "Heaven In Your Eyes," a song that would be rewritten as "I Need You Tonight" for their future album *Millennium*. Howie performed "My Heart Stays With You," which would be a B-side track on the "I Want It That Way" CD single in the UK. AJ performed "Lay Down Beside Me," another B-side track that was available on the "Quit Playing Games (With My Heart)" CD single.

The guys did a countdown to midnight and sang "Party Like It's 1999" by Prince as their encore.

BEHIND THE SCENES

During their rise in the US and Europe, there were things going on behind the scenes that didn't sit well with the group. Brian felt they weren't receiving the money they were owed. In a 2017 interview with *Entertainment Weekly*, Brian recalled coming home after doing two sold-out European tours to just $88,000 in his bank account.

"That was more [money] than I'd ever seen in my life, but on the other hand, why wasn't it three or four times that?" he said. "Then I started doing the math."

Brian hired a lawyer to look into the money the group was making. The group brought home barely $300,000 total—a little over $12,000 each per year over the preceding five years. Brian went on to sue Lou Pearlman, claiming the group had made $10 million between 1993 and 1997.

When Lou Pearlman launched the group, he had set up a shareholder's agreement that essentially made him the "sixth" Backstreet Boy. He'd earn one-sixth of what the group made. He had also encouraged the group to sign management and recording agreements with Trans Continental, which gave his company 43 percent of their revenue for "consulting services." The Boys had also given Lou Pearlman and his company, Transcontinental, power of attorney so that he, or a representative from his company, could act on the Backstreet Boys' behalf in making decisions.

The following year, in May 1998, Kevin, Howie, and AJ followed Brian's lead and sued Pearlman. Nick chose not to join the others in the lawsuit, which was settled in October 1998. Details of the settlement were never disclosed. The Boys also left Transcontinental and cut ties with Johnny and Donna Wright as their managers.

"Nobody knows what we really went through for a year, but we've all grown up a lot in the last year, and we've all matured and become businessmen," AJ told *MuchMusic* in May 1999. "It's definitely beneficial to us because we understand things in every department now. We understand now, and we're not getting the wool pulled over our eyes anymore."

During their legal battles with Lou Pearlman, the group never stopped focusing on their music careers, but more turmoil was brewing.

For one, Brian had suffered from a heart murmur from a young age and nearly died

from a bacterial infection when he was five. After getting a yearly check-up in 1997, doctors found out that his heart was larger than it should be. According to a May 1999 *Rolling Stone* article, Brian had a heart the size of a "300-pound linebacker." Because of their busy touring schedule, Brian had twice put off having surgery.

On May 8, 1998, just a week after finishing up a series of Grad Nite performances for high school seniors at Walt Disney World in Orlando, Brian underwent two-and-a-half-hour open heart surgery.

"I'll never forget when they came into the room the morning of the surgery to put me on the gurney to take me down. I just burst into tears," Brian said in the 2012 documentary, *The Heart of the Matter*. "I'll never forget looking up at the light, seeing the hospital lights in the hospital. Just not knowing if I'll wake up. It was tough. It was probably the hardest time in my life."

While Brian's surgery gave the Boys their first excuse for a vacation in three years, they were back on stage eight weeks later, kicking off their *Backstreet's Back* tour in Charlotte, North Carolina. Crews had oxygen tanks on the side of the stage, waiting for Brian in case he needed them.

Weeks later, just after the Backstreet Boys won their first MTV Video Music

ABOVE: The Boys perform during the Backstreet's Back Tour in 1998.

Cara and Brian after Z100's Jingle Ball 2005 in New York City.

BACKSTREET ARMY, ASSEMBLE!

When I think of my relationship with BSB, I think of all the time I've spent waiting. Waiting for a song to come on the radio so I could record it for a mixtape; to see if a certain music video made it to No. 1 on *TRL*; on hold on the phone to buy concert tickets; then on hold with radio stations trying to win concert tickets when they sold out; for albums to drop; for hiatuses to end; and, of course, in countless lines. SO. MANY. LINES. In 2005 all that time, money, and teen angst spent paid off when I finally met the Boys for the first time. To this day, nothing and no one has the power to instantly lift my mood the way BSB does. The escape, peace, and joy Backstreet gives me, whether it's front row at a show or through my headphones, is pure magic. Looking forward to the next thirty years, Boys!

....

CARA DONALDSON ★ PHILADELPHIA, PA
KEEPING THE BACKSTREET PRIDE ALIVE SINCE '97

Award, Howie found out that his sister, Caroline, had been rushed to the hospital in North Carolina. Caroline had been diagnosed with lupus, an autoimmune disease, in 1985, at the age of twenty-four.

Two days later, after a phone call from his brother that he should get to North Carolina, Howie arrived at the hospital. According to an article in the April 2001 edition of *Teen People*, Caroline's condition worsened an hour after Howie made it to the hospital, and doctors couldn't resuscitate her. She passed away, having lost her battle with lupus. Caroline was buried four days later in North Carolina. Three hours after the funeral, Howie was on a plane to Buenos Aires in South America for a concert.

To top off all the trials and tribulations they had been through, they lost another important person in their life: producer and songwriter Denniz PoP, who had helped the Backstreet Boys create their sound. The man who had co-written "We've Got It Goin' On," their first single, died in August 1998 of cancer.

"That year was a real soul-searching year for all of us," Howie said in the group's *Behind the Music* VH1 special in 2005. Despite these hardships, the group did achieve a lot in 1998. Besides fully breaking into the American market and their

The idea for the music video, which featured the group dressed as monsters as a throwback to Michael Jackson's "Thriller," was met with doubt by the record label. Jive thought MTV would laugh at the group. The guys had to put in their own money for the video—over $1 million dollars.

MTV Music Award for the "Everybody" video, the Backstreet Boys won their first *Billboard* Music Award for Group Album (for *Backstreet Boys*), the World's Best-Selling Dance Artist award at the World Music Awards, and the Best Non-British Act at the Smash Hit Poll Winners awards, among others.

Even with the health scares, deaths, and lawsuits, the Backstreet Boys carried on and focused on the future, including recording the new album they had begun working on in the fall of 1998—the first that would be the same around the world.

BELOW: Backstreet Boys receive keys to the city of Orlando from Mayor Glenda Hood on October 7, 1998, for raising $250,000 during a charity concert held for victims of tornadoes that struck central Florida earlier that year.

4
LARGER THAN LIFE

"The changing landscape in music—the cultural shift to happy, positive music—[the Backstreet Boys have] spearheaded that for the music industry. [The new record sales] is the best possible headline for the music industry as a whole."

—Barry Weiss, Jive Records President (1991–2011) ★
Los Angeles Times, May 27, 1999

The Boys won the Viewers' Choice Award at the 1999 MTV Music Video Awards. They took the stage at the Metropolitan Opera House in New York to accept the award.

TELL ME WHY

With new management, The Firm, who represented the likes of Leonardo DiCaprio and Jennifer Lopez, the Backstreet Boys were ready for the next step in their career—the first album that would be released around the world at the same time. They started 1999 with their first Grammy nomination for Best New Artist. However, they lost to Lauryn Hill.

Amid lawsuits and changing management, the group had begun working on their next album, *Millennium*, the year before in Stockholm, Orlando, and New York. Following the success of their second international release and first US release,

Jive Records released hidden previews of three tracks from the upcoming Backstreet Boys album on an up-and-coming new singer's debut. Fans who bought Britney Spears' . . . *Baby One More Time* were teased with three songs: "The One," "Show Me The Meaning Of Being Lonely," and "I Need You Tonight," the song previously known as "Heaven In Your Eyes." The previews were introduced by Britney Spears herself.

The same three songs were also hidden tracks on the Backstreet Boys' *A Night Out with the Backstreet Boys*. The acoustic show was performed in March 1998 for a German network but was released internationally. The songs were also previewed by Howie and Kevin on the "All I Have to Give" CD single.

RIGHT: The release of *Millennium* was exciting news for fans around the world. The Boys promoted the new album at a press conference at New York's iconic Studio 54 in May 1999.

Yet none of the teases for new music featured the song that would end up being the first single.

"I Want It That Way," another Max Martin masterpiece, co-written with Andreas Carlsson, was released internationally on April 12, 1999.

"The song is a model of melodic efficiency, with each verse building slowly and inexorably to the gently harmonized chorus," said J.D. Considine in the May 18, 1999, edition of the *Baltimore Sun*. "It may lack lyrical depth, but it has the sort of hook that will leave even the most casual listener humming happily."

"I Want It That Way" was an instant success. In the US, the song became the Backstreet Boys' fourth Top 10 single and peaked at No. 6 on the *Billboard* Hot 100 chart. It went to No. 1 on the US Adult Contemporary, US Mainstream Top 40, and US Top 40 Track charts. The success wasn't just in the United States—it went No. 1 in more than sixteen other countries. The single alone went five times platinum in Australia, triple platinum in the United States and Japan, and double platinum

Nick worked with the legendary Stan Lee (of Marvel fame) to create *The Backstreet Project*, a comic book that featured the group members as superheroes. Action figures were released through Burger King kids' meals, along with CDs and a live concert VHS called *For the Fans*.

in the United Kingdom, Sweden, and Denmark, on top of single platinum and gold status in other countries.

Did you know that the version of "I Want It That Way" that we all know and love almost wasn't released? As everyone knows, the lyrics to "I Want It That Way" make no sense. Which way do they want it? And how exactly are they two worlds apart? The only lyrics that make any sense in the song come in Kevin's bridge.

According to Andreas Carlsson, in an interview with *Billboard* about the song's twentieth anniversary in 2019, the guys and the label were unsure of the song because of the lyrics.

BELOW: This *Doonesbury* comic strip from August 6, 1999, mentioned "I Want It That Way."

"The band and the record company heard it, and they immediately said, 'This is a classic,'" Carlsson continues. "But they weren't sure about the lyrics because they thought they were too abstract—and rightfully so!"

The group went on to film a music video for the song, but Jive still had doubts about the lyrics. Songwriter Mutt Lange was flown to Sweden to rewrite the song with Max Martin. Mutt Lange would replace lyrics such as "I never wanna hear you say" with "I love it when I hear you say." The song made more sense, but in the end, the guys wanted the original version to be released. The alternate version would leak online years later as "No Goodbyes."

The music video, directed by Wayne Isham, was filmed at Los Angeles International Airport on April 1, 1999, and features real fans at the end of the video, cheering the guys on as they leave on a huge plane. JoJo Wright, a 102.7 KIIS FM Los Angeles radio DJ, announced on air that a Jive Records executive requested fifty extras to be in the music video. They required the extras to be sixteen years or older, be willing to work eight to ten hours, and bring shirts and signs.

The video debuted on *TRL* on May 5, 1999, and was No. 1 a total of forty-seven times during its sixty-five-day run on the countdown. Twenty years later, in the era of the digital world, "I Want It That Way" was certified three times platinum on April 12, 2019, for digital sales and streaming. The guys were presented with a plaque during their Larger Than Life Las Vegas residency that same day. The music video hit one billion views on YouTube on November 13,

2021. It is currently the only Backstreet Boys music video to reach this milestone.

"I remember I couldn't wait for the video to premiere on MTV," Rachael from Kentucky said. "The date was on my calendar as soon as I heard when. May 5, 1999, couldn't come soon enough. I don't think I really realized what an iconic song it was going to be."

THE COUNTDOWN IS ON

In May of 1999, the Backstreet Boys were literally everywhere.

Whether it was a music countdown show in Canada, a variety show in the United Kingdom or Germany, or a TV show in the United States, they were on television and the radio at any given moment of the day. Jive Records threw the Backstreet Boys into promotion for their new album, *Millennium*.

While the group was originally supposed to record a Disney special in May 1998 for the Disney Channel, they had to back out due to Brian's heart surgery. They got a second chance with *Backstreet Boys in Concert*, which was recorded at the New Amsterdam Theatre in New York City on May 11, 1999. It aired on the Disney Channel for the first time on July 10, 1999, and became so popular it was re-aired ten more times over the next two years.

At the same time, the Backstreet Boys also began a huge campaign with Sears, the department store. On top of advertisements in magazines and newspapers and flyers in stores and the mail, Sears held a contest to win a shopping

Lori poses with the Backstreet Boys during their Hollywood Walk of Fame ceremony, at which she introduced the group.

BACKSTREET ARMY, ASSEMBLE!

Imagine being a child and having your life altered by five people you haven't even met yet. I was only eleven when the Backstreet Boys did that for me. By thirteen, I was in their "I Want It That Way" music video. I thought I'd reached my peak, and nothing could top that. I was wrong. By some miracle, I gave one of the induction speeches when they received their star on the Hollywood Walk of Fame. Back then, I said they'd been there for me, from braces to bridal showers. That's still true. Through every milestone, they've been a source of joy, my primary coping mechanism, and my escape. They're intertwined in some of my best memories. What others could've easily dismissed as a phase has proven to be an ongoing, decades-long journey. Aside from family, they've been the most consistent presence in my life. The impact they've had on me led me to pursue a career in psychology so I could help others, too, though on a smaller scale. I wouldn't be who I am today without their influence. I'm eternally grateful I found them at that pivotal age, and I've carried them with me every day since.

LORI W. ★ LOS ANGELES, CA
KEEPING THE BACKSTREET PRIDE ALIVE SINCE '97

spree with "your favorite Backstreet Boy" and four front row seats to the Boys' show in Tampa, FL. Plus, if you spent thirty-five dollars in the juniors, cosmetics, footwear, or girls' department, you got a free Backstreet Boys poster. The group, along with Sears, also created a "Larger Than Life" award for different students around the country to celebrate their work improving their communities. Each winner would receive tickets and backstage passes to a show near them and a cash prize.

The Backstreet Boys shot a series of commercials touting the shopping spree contest. A few of the commercials paid homage to The Beatles' classic "A Hard Day's Night" by having fans chase the Boys through the streets of New York City and, of course, a Sears store.

In the US, the Backstreet Boys were invited to perform on *Saturday Night Live* for a second time, having just been the musical act nearly a year before. They did appearances on *The Rosie O'Donnell Show* and Nickelodeon's *All That*; England's *Fully Booked, The Pop Zone*, and *Top of the Pops*; Germany's *VIVA*; Canada's *MuchMusic*; and more.

The most creative thing Jive Records did to help promote *Millennium* was a series of solo commercials with each of the Backstreet Boys with the slogan, "The countdown is on!" leading up to the release date, May 18, 1999. Nick swung on a vine in a jungle, Kevin rode a jeep with a surfboard through the desert (because that makes sense!), Howie ran from the bulls in Spain, AJ dressed up as a member of the Queen's Guard in London, and Brian was an ancient gladiator.

But one of the biggest and most memorable pieces of promotion that the Backstreet Boys did came the weekend before *Millennium* was released. MTV aired a special called *Backstreet Boys Live* that was broadcast live from the MTV studios with Carson Daly hosting. They invited fans into the studio, and all five guys were there to talk about the new album, play games, perform, and more during the two-hour special.

Things got pretty crazy—and it wouldn't be the last time.

Times Square in New York City, where the MTV studios were located, had to be shut down due to the number of fans who packed the sidewalks and streets outside the studios. There were thousands— nearly ten thousand, to be exact. The frenzy outside the studios happened again two days later when the Backstreet Boys arrived at MTV the day that *Millennium* was released.

"The police came and asked us to lower the studio blinds because kids were backing up traffic," former MTV production assistant Bob Kusbit told *Vulture* in 2017. "We all looked at each other in amazement."

According to Marc Pollack in a May 1999 article in the *Hollywood Reporter*,

> In 2021, *Rolling Stone* listed "I Want It That Way" at No. 240 on their list of the 500 Greatest Songs of All Time.

OPPOSITE: On September 19, 1999, Howie performs at the MCI Center in Washington, DC, during the Into the Millennium Tour.

MTV said it reached more than nine million Backstreet Boys fans the weekend leading up to the release of *Millennium*, with special programming that continued throughout the week.

ALL OF YOUR TIME SPENT KEEPS US ALIVE

In big cities, fans waited at record shops for the release of the Backstreet Boys' latest album as the clock struck midnight on May 18, 1999.

Millennium sold 1,134,00 copies in the first week, according to SoundScan figures. For comparison, Garth Brooks' album, *Double Live*, had sold 1,085,373 copies the week of November 22, 1998. According to an article on *Yahoo! Music*, 500,000 copies of *Millennium* were sold on the very first day. The album was No. 1 on the *Billboard* 200 chart for five consecutive weeks before being knocked down a spot by Limp Bizkit. But after just three weeks, they were back at the No. 1 spot. The album was No. 1 for ten non-consecutive weeks and stayed on the chart for ninety-three weeks.

After just three months, *Millennium* sold 4.7 million copies in the US, and by December, they had sold 9.4 million copies. This made *Millennium* one of the best-selling albums of 1999 in the US alone.

Around the world, the album reached No. 1 in seventeen countries, including Austria, Canada, Denmark, Finland, Germany, Iceland, Italy, Malaysia, the Netherlands, New Zealand, Norway, Portugal, Spain, Sweden, Switzerland, and China. It reached No. 2 in Australia, Belgium, Hungary, and the UK, while in France it reached No. 8, in Japan No. 6 and in Scotland No. 4.

Millennium went on to sell 24 million copies worldwide, making it the best-selling Backstreet Boys album and one of the best-selling albums of all time.

The Backstreet Boys launched a tour in support of their new album called Into the Millennium—a tour that would take them all over Europe and North America with 123 dates. Sears sponsored the tour in North America.

The North American leg was announced on August 4, 1999, and would go on sale on August 14, 1999. At that time, it wasn't common to put an entire tour on sale on the same day. Tickets for the North American dates sold out the very same day they went on sale. That's right—all 765,000 tickets sold out on August 14, 1999. In response, thirteen more shows were added in twelve cities. The tour grossed an estimated $30 million, based on the mid-priced tickets that sold for $28 and $38. A majority of the tickets sold out in an hour, with some dates selling out in less than twenty minutes.

The tour began in Europe on June 2, 1999, and ran until September 7, 1999, when the Boys headed back to North America. The tour had one minor setback during the North American leg, which postponed a few dates. Due to Hurricane Floyd, which impacted Florida, the first two shows in Ft. Lauderdale on September 14 and 15 had to be postponed. They were rescheduled for December 5 and 6 of that year.

The February 19, 2000, show at the

now-demolished Georgia Dome in Atlanta, GA, was the biggest indoor concert in Georgia history and became the fifth most attended concert in American history. More than seventy thousand concert seats sold out in less than two hours, back in the days of standing in line or calling on the phone for tickets.

The tour won a Pollstar Concert Industry Award for Most Creative Stage Production. The stage itself was in the shape of a pentagon and was placed in the center of the venue so that the concert was "in the round," which was different than most stage setups for a tour. The stage also featured a pentagonal outer track with five ramps that reached a central, circular platform. The center platform would lower so that the band could go under the stage for wardrobe changes. The setup also allowed the Backstreet Boys to stand on

hoverboards (that were attached with wire harnesses) and fly over the audience until they reached the stage.

The second single off *Millennium*, "Larger Than Life," was co-written by Brian and Max Martin. "Larger Than Life" was originally set to be the first single off the album until the group recorded "I Want It That Way." Still, "Larger Than Life" wasn't just a normal song—it had a special meaning behind it.

"It's a thank you to the fans for all they've done for us," Howie told *Twist Magazine* in their August 1999 edition. "They're there for us through our ups and downs. This is an anthem to them for that. To us, they are larger than life."

The song would go on to be a Top 10 hit in fourteen countries around the world. It became a No. 1 hit in Hungary and No. 5 on the European Hot 100 Singles chart. In the US, it peaked at No.

ABOVE: The Boys during the Millennium Tour, 1999.

The Boys perform at the 42nd Annual Grammy Awards on February 23, 2000.

25 on the *Billboard* Hot 100, No. 6 on the Mainstream Top 40, No. 17 on Rhythmic radio, and No. 12 on The Top 40 Tracks charts. On MTV's *TRL*, the music video reached No. 1 a record fifty-seven times. No other music video spent that many days at the No. 1 spot.

The music video was filmed over a two-day period between August 12 and 14, 1999, at a soundstage at Universal Studios in Orlando. Joseph Kahn was the director of the video, his second Backstreet Boys video after "Everybody (Backstreet's Back)." The video would also be the most expensive video made at that time—production costs totaled $2.1 million.

MTV was on the set of the music video for a *Backstreet TV* special that aired live on August 12, 1999. Brian was not present as he was filming his part of the music video.

In October 1999, it was reported that attorneys for the Backstreet Boys claimed that Jive Records had breached its contract with the group and that they were no longer on the label. A month later, things changed.

In November, Jive Records signed the Backstreet Boys to a five-album, $60-million record contract. It was said to be one of the largest record deals ever. The group would also get a significant amount of money upfront. According to the *Hollywood Reporter*, they would also receive more than 20 percent of all royalties.

"The contract puts Backstreet Boys in the same financial stratum as such multimillion-dollar artists as Prince, Michael Jackson, and the Rolling Stones," Marc Pollack of *Billboard* reported in the November 16, 1999, edition of the *Daily Herald*.

YOUR EVERY WISH WILL BE DONE

Backstreet Boys released their third single off *Millennium*, a ballad called "Show Me the Meaning of Being Lonely," on December 10, 1999.

"[The song] digs its melodic claws into your skull on the first listen—it's the swooniest blending of five vocalists' timbres to date, and mighty pretty besides," *Rolling Stone* writer Arion Berger said in a 1999 album review.

The song became another hit for the Boys, reaching the Top 10 in many countries. In the US, it peaked at No. 6 on the *Billboard* Hot 100 on March 18, 2000. It reached No. 1 on *Billboard*'s Top 40 Mainstream chart and also reached No. 1 in Canada.

The music video for the song was filmed between December 11 and 12, 1999. The video has a more mature, somewhat darker feel than most of their videos. Each member has their own story to tell in the video. At the beginning, a message appears stating that the video is dedicated to Denniz PoP, the producer who passed away in 1998, as well as to anyone who has lost a loved one.

It starts off with Brian in the hospital, looking at doctors trying to save a patient. Brian himself portrays the patient. His scene in the video was a reference to his open-heart surgery in May 1998. In the next scene, AJ is holding a picture of a girl. The girl represents an old friend of his who died in a car accident when she was fifteen. The bus he rides in the video says Denniz St., another tribute to the late Denniz PoP. The driver of the bus also resembles Denniz PoP.

Kevin reflected on the loss of his father when he was nineteen, watching home video footage in the music video. Many wondered if the footage was of his actual father, but in the "Millennium 20 Edition" of the video, available on the Backstreet Boys YouTube channel, Kevin explains that he is watching actors that portray him and his father.

In the scene with Nick, he saves a woman who is nearly hit by a bus. In Howie's, a woman runs toward him and fades away as she gets closer to him. The woman represents his sister, Caroline, who passed away in September 1998.

The video premiered on MTV's New Year's Eve 1999 show and was the last music video shown on MTV in the twentieth century. The music video was another staple on the *TRL* countdown starting on January 4, 2000. It spent sixty-five days on the countdown, and twenty-one of those days were at No. 1.

By the end of 1999, the Boys had racked up numerous awards for *Millennium*. At the *Billboard* Music Awards, they received four awards for the album— Album of the Year, Albums Artists/

ABOVE: The Boys pose backstage during the 1999 MTV Music Awards Party at Lincoln Center in New York.

Duo/Group of the Year, Albums Artist of the Year, and Artist of the Year. One of the Smash Hits Poll Winners awards that they won was for Best Single of 1999, for "I Want It That Way."

They were even winners of the 1999 *Rolling Stone* Readers Poll. They won Artists of the Year, Band of the Year, Album of the Year, Single of the Year, Best Video, Best Dressed, Best Fan Site, Best Tour, *and* Biggest Hype. This led them to be featured in the January 2000 issue of the magazine. The cover of the magazine featured the famous photo of the guys with their pants down.

BACKSTREET'S GRAMMY NOMINATIONS

On January 4, 2000, the 42nd Annual Grammy Awards nominees were announced, and the Backstreet Boys were nominated for four awards: Record of the Year ("I Want It That Way"), Album of the Year, Song of the Year (which is given to the songwriters), and Pop Performance by a Duo or Group ("I Want It That Way.")

The awards ceremony took place on February 23, 2000, at the Staples Center in Los Angeles. The Backstreet Boys were in attendance and performed not once but twice. They performed with Elton John on the song "Philadelphia Freedom." Their other performance was a medley of hits, including the Bee Gees' "How Deep Is Your Love," The Temptations' "Papa Was a Rolling Stone," and Boyz II Men's "I'll Make Love To You." Right after the medley, they sang their own song, "Show Me The Meaning of Being Lonely."

Unfortunately, the group left the ceremony without an award. The band Santana, nominated in the same categories, won all four awards. This caused great upset amongst the Backstreet Army, and to this day, fans still believe that the Backstreet Boys should have won.

And they should have.

I'LL BE THE ONE

The fourth and final single from *Millennium* would be a fan-chosen single, as announced on *TRL* in early March. The song choices were "Don't Want You Back," "The One," and "It's Got to Be You."

On March 8, 2000, Nick called into *TRL* to talk about the poll with Carson Daly. When Nick called in, "Don't Want You Back" was leading with 44 percent of the vote, "It's Gotta Be You" was at 30 percent, and "The One" was last at 27 percent. Carson asked if Nick had a preference; Nick did.

"We were throwing around ideas for videos and stuff, and maybe this might persuade them to change their mind," Nick told Carson live on the air. "'I'll Be The One' is the one I was thinking about and some of the other guys like. We were thinking about doing an old western-type video, like *Blazing Saddles*." The moment fans heard Nick liked "The One," they rushed to MTV's website and voted for that song instead. The final results were revealed on March 10, and "The One" had won the poll, with 37 percent of the votes, making it the next single. It just narrowly beat "Don't Want You Back," which earned 36 percent of the votes. "It's Gotta Be You" came in with 27 percent. Every now and then, the other guys still give Nick a hard time about it.

The single was released on May 16, 2000. "The One" was another Max Martin penned track; Brian also wrote on the track. The song managed to peak at just No. 30 on the *Billboard* Hot 100 in the US and No. 11 on the Mainstream Top 40. Worldwide, the single fared better, reaching the Top 10 in eleven countries.

Fans never got that western video for "The One." The music video that *was* released for the song would be the first video they did not film themselves.

OPPOSITE: Howie poses with Sir Elton John at the party following a special VIP screening of *The Road to El Dorado* in Los Angeles, California, in 2000.

Instead, the Boys used footage from their Into the Millennium Tour and behind-the-scenes footage from 1999 and 2000. The video was co-directed by Kevin and Chris Hafner. Kevin used some of his own footage from tour rehearsals and other excursions. The video opens with a message dedicating the video to fans, their crew, the band, and the dancers for a wonderful year.

NEW ALBUM IN THE WORKS

Backstreet Boys and Burger King launched a five-week promotion, beginning August 28, 2000, that included commercials, three live CDs, a VHS, and action figures from their Backstreet Project comic book.

The three live CDs also included a brand-new song from their next album, *Black & Blue*, called "It's True." The CDs could also be played on a computer, where fans could take quizzes and make scrapbooks with photos and quotes. Screensavers and wallpapers could also be downloaded from the CD.

The forty-five-minute VHS included interviews with the guys and behind-the-scenes footage, along with concert footage. The live tracks and video footage were recorded at their Indianapolis, Indiana, concert in March 2000.

Fans could purchase the CDs and VHS with any meal for just $2.99. The action figures were included with a kids' meal.

Three commercials were also filmed for the promotion. One of the commercials, entitled "The Deal," shows the guys in a conference room with the head of Burger King, who offers them a deal to have them appear at a Burger King and do a commercial. The group declines, saying they don't do commercials. But then they're offered a lifetime supply of Burger King Whoppers; the next shot is the Boys performing the Burger King jingle, "Have It Your Way." Another commercial features the guys performing on stage, in a limo, and on their tour bus with a Burger King worker popping up everywhere to give them Whoppers. The last commercial was geared toward kids, promoting the kids' meal featuring their action figures.

Three of the guys are eating at Burger King, and young kids see them and run to them. Suddenly, the guys transform into their comic book characters and run off. In the end, the guys are all seated together to say kids rule.

The Backstreet Boys spent the summer of 2000 recording a brand-new album that was set for a fall release. During an interview with CBS' *The Early Show* that aired in May 2000, Nick, Howie, and Kevin were in the studios in the Bahamas. Both Kevin and Howie previewed two new songs. One of them was the song "What Makes You Different (Makes

In the "Millennium 20 Edition" of the video on the Boys' YouTube channel, Nick is quoted about the *TRL* poll: "The guys blame me to this day for swaying the public vote!"

You Beautiful)," which would go on to be featured on the soundtrack for the movie *The Princess Diaries* in 2001 and would also appear as a bonus track on their album in some countries.

In the interview, Kevin spoke about why he enjoyed recording in the Bahamas: "It's just a great vibe. I mean, when you're feeling like you got writer's block or something, you can walk out the front door and walk right out on the beach, and with a tape recorder and a pen and pad and just let it come out."

During a surprise visit to *TRL* on June 12, 2000, AJ spoke about the new album,

stating that they were only writing songs at that time and that the album would incorporate rock, R&B, hip-hop, and country influences. AJ also mentioned that Nick and Kevin would play the drums and piano on the album.

Then, in July, it was off to Sweden to record and work with Max Martin. The group would spend July through September 2000 recording new music for the album. With this album, they got the opportunity to write more than they had in the past, though only five out of the seven songs they had written would end up being on the album.

ABOVE: Another photo from the *Millennium* press conference at Studio 54. The Boys are joined by Sears Director of Event Marketing, John Lebbad.

5

BLACK & BLUE

"Backstreet Boys have found longevity—or at least extended their life expectancy—through a kind of youthful earnestness. Ten years from now, Backstreet Boys won't look or sound quite as goofy or dated as New Kids on the Block."

—Jordan Zivitz ★ *Calgary Herald,* November 18, 2000

The Backstreet Boys perform at the Pepsi Center in Denver, Colorado, on October 10, 2001.

LONELINESS IS TRAGICAL

After three months of recording, the Backstreet Boys released the first single from their next album, *Black & Blue*, but they had a tremendous amount of pressure on their backs. *NSYNC had released their second album, *No Strings Attached*, that March and had broken the Boys' SoundScan album sales record—by a *lot*. The album sold over 2.4 million copies in the first week alone, shattering the Backstreet Boys' *Millennium* record.

The first single off *Black & Blue* was "Shape of My Heart" and was released on October 2, 2000. The mid-tempo single, another Max Martin hit, was also written with Rami and Lisa Miskovsky. It became a No. 1 hit in Canada, Europe, Italy, New Zealand, Norway, Sweden, Switzerland, and the UK. It went to No. 9 in the US on the *Billboard* Hot 100 but went to No. 2 on the US Adult Contemporary chart.

"'Shape of My Heart,' the current single, is typical, with a slightly soulful verse (supported by acoustic guitar and quietly pulsing synths) exploding into a big, ABBA-esque chorus," J.D. Considine said of the song in the November 27, 2000, edition of the *Kenosha News*. "It may be no more substantial than meringue, but it's also as tasty, with a fluffy sweetness that will leave pop fans hungry for more."

The music video was set in blue tones and was filmed at the Orpheum Theatre in Los Angeles. It features the band watching actors rehearsing and also interacting with the actors. It became an instant hit on *TRL*, breaking the group's own record for the longest-running No. 1 video (previously held by "Larger Than Life"). The video for "Shape of My Heart" spent sixty-one days out of sixty-five at the No. 1 spot. No other artist broke that record, as *TRL* later changed the limit of how long a video could be on the countdown.

With the release of a new single and an upcoming album, the Backstreet Boys went on a media spree, filming interviews and performances all over the world, including appearances on *TRL*, a special edition of *Making The Video* for "Shape of My Heart," *Top of the Pops*, *Wetten, dass..?*, *eUK*, and more before *Black & Blue* was released.

Fans around the country and the world worked to help *Black & Blue*'s album sales skyrocket. According to the December 8, 2000, edition of the *Kansas City Star*, local fans were a part of "BSB-OOST" (Backstreet Boys Official Online Street Team) to help get the word out. More than sixteen thousand members helped promote the album, whether it was in person by creating T-shirts to wear to school or on Backstreet Boys chat rooms, forums, and webpages.

AROUND THE WORLD ... IN ONE HUNDRED HOURS?

The one hundred-hour, around-the-world media tour to support *Black & Blue* started in Stockholm, right after the MTV Europe Music Awards, and made stops in Tokyo, Sydney, Cape Town, and Rio de Janeiro

before the Boys made their way back to New York City. That meant they spent around fifty-five hours in the air and forty-five hours on the ground promoting the new album.

The Backstreet Boys won Best Group at the MTV Europe Music Awards, and the next morning, they boarded the plane in Stockholm, waving to adoring fans from the tarmac like The Beatles in clips from the '60s. The Boys landed in Tokyo to what they thought were crickets, but as they made their way through the airport, they saw that wasn't the case. There were a couple of thousand fans. Police had barricaded aisles so the Backstreet Boys

could make their way to the buses for press and to make appearances for fans. They spent twelve hours in Tokyo.

The next stop in Sydney, Australia, was a bit calmer. While it was November and cold in North America, it was summertime down under. The Boys made their way to the beach, where they were welcomed by lifeguards in swimsuits and Speedos with custom surfboards for the Boys. The group was in Australia for thirteen hours. They spent only five hours on the ground in Cape Town, South Africa, next, but it was the Boys' first trip there, and the first time some fans would get to see them in person, so it was still a momentous event.

ABOVE: The Boys land in Australia during their world tour to promote *Black & Blue* in November 2000.

The "dun dun dun, dun dun dun dun" break down in "The Call" is actually Howie passing gas in the recording booth. "So Max tweaked it and made it sound like one of his patented bass sounds, and it stayed on the record," AJ told *Billboard* in 2017.

The next stop on the world tour—Rio de Janeiro, Brazil—was the craziest. Fans were crowded at the airport and along the streets as the buses tried to drive to the next destination.

"We were told there were a couple of people outside the hotel at first. By the time we got around closer to the area, there was a good couple of thousand," Howie told *MTV Diary* in 2000.

Fans ran alongside the buses, banging on the windows, even trying to climb *on* the bus. Fans were crying, pushing against the authorities to get closer to the Boys. There ended up being ten thousand fans outside the hotel, and a crowd made the bus that the Backstreet Boys were on rock. The Boys eventually found a quick way to run from the bus to the hotel so that they could safely meet fans and do press.

However, the crowd outside continued to grow, and there were eventually more than forty thousand fans screaming. The Backstreet Boys decided to perform a concert on the roof of the hotel. Interestingly, Dave Grohl of the Foo Fighters was in the hotel at that same exact time.

"They put us on a balcony, and I look over, and the fucking Backstreet Boys were

singing 'I Want It That Way,' so I'm hanging over the balcony [and dancing], and one of them sees me," Dave told *Time* in 2009. "I got caught singing one of their songs."

The Backstreet Boys would end up spending eleven hours on the ground in Rio before jetting off to New York for the actual release of the album. Back in the States, fans lined the tarmac as if the Boys were Elvis Presley leaving for the Army. But instead, fans were welcoming the group home. After a press conference where they announced a new world tour, the band made their way to the *TRL* studios. Times Square was just as packed as it had been each time they had been there before.

That night, the group performed in an MTV special called *Backstreet Over Broadway* on the roof of the MTV studios, where they performed "Shape of My Heart" acoustically for fans who had braved the cold temperatures outside. *Black & Blue* was officially released on November 21, 2000, just before Thanksgiving and the popular Black Friday shopping day.

"On 'Black & Blue,' the quintet tries to keep things fresh with slightly more mature lyrics that match their changing lives, marriages, and relationships. Chances are, their audience has grown up a bit, learning that getting a boyfriend is not the ticket to paradise our romance-obsessed culture promises," Larry Nager said in a review of

Ashley Thomas poses with the boys she loves "More Than Words" in Kansas City, Missouri, during the 2019 DNA World Tour.

BACKSTREET ARMY, ASSEMBLE!

The Backstreet Boys have been a constant source of happiness in my life. They have lifted my spirits when nothing else could. Their music has served as a source of inspiration throughout all the occasions of my life. I could not be more grateful for being a witness to their bond. They are a true brotherhood. I admire how open and honest they have always been with their fans. I love that they never shy away from telling us the truth and their dedication to giving us their best. As a self-proclaimed "AJ Girl," I could write for hours about my appreciation for him. AJ's sobriety journey is a part of his story, but it is such a small part of who he is. AJ is honest, kind, compassionate, gracious, and talented beyond measure. Having had the opportunity to meet him more than a few times, I am so happy to proclaim that my "favorite person" is everything you would want in your favorite pop star. The same can be said for the entire group. You never wonder if the Backstreet Boys care about their fans. They prove it in every interaction, appearance, and performance. Whatever comes next, count me in.

ASHLEY THOMAS ★ NASHVILLE, TN
KEEPING THE BACKSTREET PRIDE ALIVE SINCE '97

Brian and Kevin both got engaged over the Christmas holidays in 1999. Kevin married Kristin Willits in Lee County, KY, in June 2000. Brian married Leighanne Wallace in Atlanta in September 2000.

Black & Blue in the November 26, 2000, edition of the *Tennessean*.

The work of constant promotion that Nick, AJ, Brian, Kevin, and Howie did, along with the efforts of fans, paid off. The new album debuted at No. 1 on the US *Billboard* 200, selling 1.6 million copies in one week. While it didn't break the *NSYNC record, it did outsell *Millennium*. The Backstreet Boys became the first act in history to sell more than one million copies of albums in the first week with back-to-back releases.

The album also went No. 1 in Canada, Germany, Malaysia, Spain, and Switzerland and was a Top 3 album in nine other countries. According to a November 29, 2000, article at *SoundSpike*, *Black & Blue* had the most sales in a week internationally for any album in history, selling more than five million copies. A DVD release of the Boys' one hundred–hour world media tour, *Around the World*, also ended up going platinum after its release.

DON'T WAIT UP FOR ME

With *Black & Blue* released and the holiday season over, it was time for the second single from the album—"The Call."

"The Call," yet another excellent Max Martin/Rami entry, was the Backstreet Boys' first single that hinted at adulthood. The song

was about a man who is being unfaithful to his girlfriend and calls her to let her know he'll be home late (after he meets another woman at a bar). The song wasn't the strongest hit on the charts, only having gone to No. 1 on the UK Indie charts and in Romania, but the song still remains a favorite among fans even today, especially live in concert.

The music video was shot in Los Angeles and featured each of the Boys being chased or haunted by a woman that they were cheating on. Filming included long night shoots—and that was when AJ would try cocaine for the first time.

"First time I tried cocaine was the night we shot 'The Call' video, and I made a point to tell everybody on set that I was on coke because I was paranoid," AJ said in VH1's *Behind The Music* special in 2005.

According to AJ, when he talked to Oprah Winfrey about that night in a 2003 interview, each of the Boys had a different call time for a night shoot since they shot individually and only shot one scene together for the very end of the video.

"I went out that night for my solo shot, had a couple of drinks that night. Came back to my hotel room and passed out for an hour. Had to wake up, and I was completely groggy," AJ told Oprah. A friend that was with him suggested he do a bump of cocaine to perk him up.

The video premiered on *TRL* on January 17, 2001, and the next day, it debuted on the

ABOVE: Howie and Nick perform in Orlando for the start of the second leg of the Black & Blue World Tour on June 8, 2001.

countdown at No. 2. It spent fifty-four days at No. 1, with a total of sixty-five days on the countdown before it was retired on April 30, 2001.

INSIDE THE CIRCUS

The day that *Black & Blue* was released, the Backstreet Boys released tour dates for their upcoming 2001 Black & Blue World Tour, and it was expected to be huge. The Boys were slated to play the United States and Canada before heading to Mexico and South America. Then the tour would come back to the United States before heading to Europe, the Pacific Rim, Japan, Australia, and New Zealand.

"This is the richest touring deal in music history, relative to the guarantees the group is receiving versus the ticket prices they are charging and the capacities they're playing," SFX Touring Vice President Bruce Kapp said in the December 20, 2000, edition of the *Index-Journal*. "It's gonna be huge."

The tour kicked off in their home state of Florida on January 22, 2001, in Sunrise, and reviews were positive. "The songs from the group's latest album, 'Black and Blue,' worked surprisingly well in concert, lending a dash of maturity to the setlist," Shane Harrison said in the January 28, 2001, edition of the *Atlanta Constitution*. "When you could hear from above the leather-lunged fans, the Boys provided a slick but satisfying evening's entertainment."

The Backstreet Boys pose for photos in Stockholm, Sweden, before taking off on a one hundred-hour promotional trip for *Black & Blue*, on November 17, 2000.

ABOVE: Though the Boys couldn't do the 2001 Super Bowl halftime show (they had just started their Black & Blue Tour), they did get to perform the national anthem before football's biggest game.

By the end, they had even the beefiest guys in the stadium patriotically holding hands over hearts," a review by Gina Vivinetto said in the January 29, 2001, edition of the *Tampa Bay Times*. "Strident fireworks and a military flyover during those powerful lines about rockets' red glare and bombs bursting in the air made the Boys' rendition one of the finest in recent memory."

"MORE THAN THAT"

The day after the show in Atlanta at the Georgia Dome was the 2001 Super Bowl, and the group had been offered the halftime show. Because the tour had just begun, they didn't have time to create a show and be in Tampa for the rehearsals. The halftime show went to *NSYNC (there they are again, getting BSB's leftovers), Britney Spears, Aerosmith, and Mary J. Blige. However, not all was lost.

When the Backstreet Boys passed on the halftime show, they were offered the national anthem.

"At the time we came from the era of, we loved the Whitney Houston rendition of the national anthem. And for us, we got the choice, and we passed on the halftime," Nick told *People* in 2021.

So on January 28, 2001, Nick's twenty-first birthday, in his hometown of Tampa, FL, the Boys performed the national anthem in Super Bowl XXXV between the Baltimore Ravens and New York Giants. "Backstreet, however, did our anthem proud. Although they had a taped musical accompaniment, the Boys performed the notoriously difficult tune live.

Jive released the third single from *Black & Blue* on April 17, 2001. "More Than That," another mid-tempo song, was recorded in Sweden and written by Adam Anders, Franciz, and LePont. It was the first single that the Backstreet Boys had released in years that did not have Max Martin's fingerprints on it.

The song reached No. 27 on the US *Billboard* 100, No. 6 on the US Adult Contemporary, and No. 14 on the US Mainstream Top 40. It went to No. 12 on the UK Singles Chart, ending its thirteenth consecutive Top 10 run. While the song didn't perform as well as other singles in certain regions, "More Than That" still went to No. 2 in Poland and No. 9 in Scotland.

The music video, directed by Marcus Raboy, featured the group in the desert in several different scenes—in a large hanger, driving in the desert in two separate cars, and walking in the sand. The video went to No. 1 on *TRL* for the first time on May 15, 2001, and was back and forth with *NSYNC's "Pop" through July and August. It was No. 1 a total of thirty-four times, with the longest streak being ten days.

GOING SOUTH

The Black & Blue World Tour continued through March, followed by a month-long break before heading to South America and Puerto Rico. While the group was on break, CBS aired a new TV special, *Backstreet Boys: Larger Than Life*, with snippets from the Black & Blue World Tour, stop in Los Angeles, along with clips from their one hundred–hour world promotional tour. The ratings were solid, with 6.33 million viewers (according to Nielsen Ratings) for the week ending June 3, 2001. To coincide with the TV special, *TV Guide* released six different covers of their May 26–June 1, 2001, issue—one with each of the Boys and one group cover.

The second leg of the Black & Blue World Tour began the next week, on June 8, 2001, with a hometown show in Orlando at the TD Waterhouse Center (now Amway Arena). But there were concerns behind the scenes. AJ had been missing rehearsals, and the other boys knew something was going on, though they didn't yet know what.

According to the Backstreet Boys' appearance on the December 10, 2003, episode of *The Oprah Winfrey Show*, Brian, Kevin, and Nick broke into AJ's house when he didn't show up to rehearsals. "That was one of the first times that it really—the intervention really took place because we saw him lying in his bed where he couldn't get out of bed," Brian said.

The tour continued, with stops along the East Coast before hitting Boston, where they had three shows at the Fleet Center. With a

day off between the second and third show, the Boys had agreed to throw out the first pitch at the Boston Red Sox game against the Atlanta Braves and to sing the national anthem, but AJ didn't want to go.

ABOVE: A shot from the Boys' whirlwind one hundred-hour trip around the world to promote Black & Blue. This was taken in Tokyo on November 18, 2000.

Kevin broke down the hotel room door to get to AJ, but AJ double-bolted the bedroom door, so Kevin couldn't get in.

"He's basically like, 'fuck you. I'm not working on my day off,'" Kevin said on *Behind the Music* in 2005. "I'm like, 'You know what, I'm done with you. I can't stand you anymore. I hate you. You make me sick. You're dead to me.'"

Nick, Brian, Howie, and Kevin attended the game as scheduled, but AJ decided to leave Boston entirely. He called his security and told them he was done and wanted to go home. The next day, he checked himself into rehab in Arizona, and the Backstreet Boys ended up making one of the hardest announcements of their career.

Kristen Whitman talks with AJ McLean in 2005 in Manhattan.

BACKSTREET ARMY, ASSEMBLE!

It is impossible to properly explain what it is to be a BSB fan. It is a lifelong love affair guaranteed to bring joy even in the most tumultuous of times. From awkward preteen to married mom, I have carried the joy of boyband fandom with me in the core of my soul. I met the Boys on a frigid night in December 2005 on a sidewalk in Manhattan, stunned beyond reason when they suddenly materialized before my eyes. I found myself in easy conversation with AJ and Nick, and at that moment, I realized they truly were who I'd always hoped they'd be: legitimately good guys who loved their fans. Now when people ask about my forever adoration, I can confidently tell them what I always knew: the Backstreet Boys loved us through the airwavevs when we didn't have the ability to love ourselves. They vowed to Never Break Our Hearts, and thirty years later, they're still upholding that promise.

KRISTEN WHITMAN ★ CONSHOHOCKEN, PA
KEEPING THE BACKSTREET PRIDE ALIVE SINCE '97

Rumors began swirling online and on message boards about the third Boston show being canceled. Fans were becoming upset, especially when an anonymous person posted that the Backstreet Boys were on their way to New York City to make an announcement.

When *TRL* began on July 9, 2001, it seemed like a normal Monday. Who would be number one? Would it be *NSYNC's "Pop" or Backstreet Boys' "More Than That"? As the countdown went on, approaching the Top 3 videos, it became more somber. Then *TRL* came back from a commercial, and Carson was in the audience. He motioned for MTV reporter John Norris, who was sitting in front of the cameras with Nick, Brian, Kevin, and Howie.

"AJ and we have come to a decision that he is going to seek treatment for depression, anxiety, and his obsessive consumption of alcohol," Kevin announced. "Initially for thirty days."

"We didn't want to lie about it. We didn't want to push it under the rug and say he was sick and broke his leg or something. We wanted to be honest with our fans," Kevin added.

"I think the hardest part of letting everybody know the truth was that we were letting ourselves know the truth at the same time," Brian told VH1's *Behind the Music* years later.

Fans were left heartbroken, not for the tour, but for AJ and the sadness that had come over their favorite group.

According to a Billboard.com article from 2020, "Shape of My Heart" is "The sound of a boy band becoming a group of men."

"I was heartbroken. He was (and still is) my favorite, and to know he was struggling with an addiction broke my heart," Penni Harris from Douglas, GA, said. "No, I did not know him personally, but he (and the guys) had been a part of my everyday life since I was fourteen. I was dumbfounded that he wasn't 'perfect' and just wanted things to be alright. I was saddened the shows would be postponed but felt, in the end, things would be alright. They just had to be."

The Backstreet Boys rescheduled their July and early August tour dates and planned to resume the Black & Blue World Tour on August 7, but on August 1, 2001, they postponed more dates so that AJ could extend his time in rehab.

The Black & Blue World Tour restarted on August 24, 2001, in Milwaukee, WI, with AJ on stage looking happy and healthier. Seven days later, the Backstreet Boys streamed their Dallas, Texas, stop live on Yahoo! for fans across the world. A few days later, they arrived in Boston again for three shows. From there, they would head to Toronto on September 11, 2001.

As history knows, 9/11 would become a traumatic day for all Americans. The group was personally affected by the tragedy when one member of their crew, Daniel Lee, was killed on American Airlines Flight 11. He was on his way home to California for the birth of his daughter. Brian's wife, Leighanne, had also planned to be on the flight but canceled the night before.

6
DROWNING

··

"As for the Backstreet Boys, make
fun of them for their pre-packed
image and cheesy videos, if you will.
You'll get no argument here. But the first
of the current boy bands has made,
by far, the most tuneful, least gimmicky,
and most enduring pop music of the lot.
Can anyone resist 'I Want It That Way'?"

—Howard Cohen ★ *The Miami Herald*, November 2, 2001

The Backstreet Boys during the 2001 MTV Video Music Awards at
Lincoln Center in New York.

THE HITS - CHAPTER ONE

Jive Records announced that the Boys would be releasing a hits compilation called *The Hits – Chapter One* on October 23, 2001. It would include singles from their previous albums and one new song called "Drowning."

Jive had decided to release a greatest hits album as they, the label, had not released a new album in 2001. The Backstreet Boys resisted. They felt it was too early in their career to release a hits album, and they had plans to release one in 2003 to coincide with the group's tenth anniversary.

"Our management company was supportive [of the Hits album], and we weren't. And the record company was going to put it out anyway," Kevin told the *New York Times* in an August 18, 2002, article. "So it's either promote, or fight with your label, don't promote it and risk it doing

BELOW: The Boys pose for photographers before a news conference in Mexico City in March 2001. They did three concerts in Mexico as part of the Black & Blue Tour.

very badly. But ultimately, who is it that's going to get hurt? It's not going to hurt our label. It's going to hurt us."

The greatest hits album would go on to debut at No. 4 on the *Billboard* 200 chart, making it the group's third album to debut in the Top 10. But sales were down compared to their previous two albums, with only 197,000 copies sold in the first week. Still, by September 2002, the album was certified platinum for selling over 1.8 million copies. Meanwhile, over in the UK, the album was certified platinum in November 2001 by BPI for shipments of 300,000 copies. The album was the thirteenth best-selling album of 2001, with shipments of 5 million worldwide.

"Drowning" was released as a single on October 16, 2001. The song had originally been recorded in 2000 for inclusion on the *Black & Blue* album. It was another Andreas Carlsson-penned track that was co-written with Rami and Linda Thompson (known for being engaged to Elvis Presley and married to Caitlyn Jenner). The single managed to reach No. 28 on the *Billboard* Hot 100. It was a Top 10 hit in over thirteen countries.

As for the music video, the Boys would film two separate videos for the song. They weren't impressed with the first version due to the CGI that was used to showcase rain, water, and other elements. The CGI was cheesy, especially when water rushed over them from a tidal wave. So, instead, they had Nigel Dick, who had filmed a few of their past videos, direct the new version of the video.

"The powers that be did not like the original version of 'Drowning,' which was

shot by someone else," Nigel Dick said on his official website. "My brief was: 'shoot some performance with beautiful photography and don't make it expensive or blue or grey or wet!'"

The video was filmed in Los Angeles and would be the last video from the Backstreet Boys to appear on MTV's *TRL* for a while. It debuted on the countdown at No. 4 on October 30, 2001. The video retired on February 26, 2002, at number 1.

NEW ALBUM?

After the release of *The Hits – Chapter One*, the Backstreet Boys began working on a new album in 2002, but the recording didn't go according to plan. There were several issues with their record label at that time—namely, the group wanted to record a new album, but Jive/Zomba wanted Nick to go solo instead.

In March 2002, the group had a meeting, as they felt they weren't getting the personal attention they deserved from their management, The Firm. Brian and AJ took the lead in deciding to part ways with The Firm. They later found out that Nick had decided to stay with The Firm and that the company would manage his solo career. The group found new management in the form of Howard Kaufman and Irving Azoff, who were industry veterans.

Kevin hosted *TRL* on April 1, 2002, where he decided to play a prank on fans by saying the group had broken up. He announced that he would be joining a punk rock band, and Nick was doing a solo album. A little later in the episode, he stated that it was an April Fool's prank. Fans weren't laughing, even if it was a joke.

With Jive Records/Zomba more interested in Nick's solo career than the next Backstreet Boys album, the other four members of the group began recording demos without Nick. Unfortunately, the album set to be released in 2002 never happened due to ongoing issues with Jive Records.

On November 25, 2002, the Backstreet Boys filed a $75-million lawsuit against the Zomba Recording Corporation, looking to also be released from their 1994 record contract. The lawsuit cited breach of contract, intentional interference with contract, trademark infringement, and unfair competition. It also stated that Zomba refused to take part in the selection of songs and producers for the album, which made it impossible to record the new album. The group was contractually barred from recording without the label's approval. Had

they been able to deliver an album by the April 30, 2002, deadline, the group would have also been entitled to a $5 million advance. The lawsuit alleged that Zomba had added a one-year delay on their next album to avoid paying the advance the Boys were owed. The lawsuit also demanded that the label stop using the Backstreet Boys' trademark name and their official website to promote Nick's solo album.

During this time, Nick released his first solo album, *Now or Never*, on October 29, 2002. He would also launch his first solo tour on February 17, 2003. Brian and his wife Leighanne welcomed a baby boy, Baylee, on November 27, 2002. Kevin took a starring role in the Broadway musical, *Chicago*, starting on January 20, 2003, until early March of the same year.

Some fans had mixed feelings about Nick going solo.

"I remember being excited for [Nick] because I loved hearing him sing, but I would be lying if I said I didn't worry about the band," Kim Schussler of Bear, DE, said. "It was a weird feeling because I knew I wanted to experience 'solo Nick' and support his endeavors, but I knew I wasn't ready for the group to 'end' yet, so to speak."

Kim's twin sister Kerry felt the same.

"At first, I felt a little uncertain because I didn't know what it meant for the future

> "All five of us went back into the studio this past February and have been working to create what we think will be our best album yet. It has been really great being back together working on our music." —Backstreet Boys statement on WEG website, April 6, 2004

The Backstreet Boys pose with fan Brianne Fleming and a flag celebrating her alma mater, the University of Central Florida, located in Orlando, where the group got their start.

BACKSTREET ARMY, ASSEMBLE!

Childhood is about discovering yourself and finding places to direct all the extra love you have in your heart. Well, all the love I had to give went to the Backstreet Boys, and it still endures today. Their music has given me purpose and something to be passionate about, but more than anything, they've given me memories. Loving the Backstreet Boys is never something I've done alone. It's something I've experienced with family, friends, my husband, and even fans on social media who I've later met in the front row at a show. No matter where I am, their music puts me in my happy place. After thirty years, they continue to show up for us, and I can't thank them enough for that. When you love the Backstreet Boys, it feels like they love you back. Their impact has stood the test of time, and I've cherished every moment.

BRIANNE FLEMING ★ DELRAY BEACH, FL
KEEPING THE BACKSTREET PRIDE ALIVE SINCE '97

of the rest of the group, but I was also very excited for him," Kerry said. "I always enjoyed when he performed solos on the tour, so I was very curious to hear an album of his own!"

After Nick's tour and Kevin's time on Broadway ended, the group planned to meet up to discuss what was next for them. In a March 17, 2003, interview, Kevin said that the group would have that meeting the following day. In a statement released on March 26, 2003, they announced that they would not be recording a new album at that time.

"We are not breaking up, but individually we are currently at different places in our lives, and our hearts and minds are focused in other areas," the statement said. "All of us are getting along great and are supporting each other in our individual endeavors. When the timing is right, we will record another Backstreet Boys album. We would like to thank our fans for their continued support and love throughout our career."

With no new album or single during these two years, and a seeming focus on solo endeavors, many believed the Boys had indeed broken up. Nick finished his first solo tour and was heavily involved in powerboat racing due to his father Bob's passion for the sport. He'd even won a championship the year before. He filmed his first movie, *The Hollow*, during the summer of 2003 and was beginning to work on a second solo album. Kevin went on tour with *Chicago*, doing shows in Pittsburgh, PA, and San Francisco, CA, and even went overseas to London. Howie and Brian did charity work and events for their respective

charities, the Dorough Lupus Foundation and the Healthy Heart Club. AJ continued to work on his sobriety while performing occasional shows in the Los Angeles area with his then fiancé.

In the meantime, AJ's mother, Denise, had written a book about her son's career and all the good and hardship it had brought. The book, *Backstreet Mom: A Mother's Tale of Backstreet Boy AJ McLean's Rise to Fame, Struggle with Addiction, and Ultimate Triumph*, was published on November 10, 2003. That same month, AJ, along with his mother, appeared on *The Oprah Winfrey Show* to discuss AJ's addiction and the new book. Neither of them knew that there would be special guests.

Just who were those special guests? The other members of the Backstreet Boys.

It had been six months since they were all together in the same room. Rather than film a video message, the guys decided to be there for AJ in person, with Nick even flying in from London, where he was working on a second solo album. Fans got to watch this moment when it aired on television on December 10, 2003.

Our five favorite guys were back together once again.

WORK IN PROGRESS

Many believed it was the moment they appeared on *The Oprah Winfrey Show* that the guys decided to record a new album. That wasn't the case. During an interview with Atlanta radio station Star 94 FM in December 2003, Brian mentioned that the

guys had been in talks a few months prior to that. He even stated that the Boys would be in the studio on January 10, 2004.

"We're all excited. All of us hadn't been together in the same room in like six months, so it was wild. It was good to be back together again," Kevin told *MTV News* in a December 3, 2003, news report. "We've got some stuff written, but we're gonna go in with an open mind and just explore and experiment and see what happens. We've been talking about going with live horn sections and stuff like that, just funkin' it up, but not really in a hip-hop sort of way. More of using horns and live strings and a little bit of a '70s edge or something. We just wanna make music that we're proud of and have fun."

The guys would also work with Max Martin once again. This time around, the sound would have a little more rock edge to it. It was something fans did not expect, but they were excited about it.

"We just got finished working with Max Martin again," AJ told *MTV News* in a June 3, 2004, report. "He kind of went into hiding for a little bit—took a little break from the pop world and had a baby. And we caught wind through our record company that there was a song he wrote that he thought would be cool for us to try."

Brian also spoke about the different styles they were experimenting with. "It's got urban, it's got pop, it's got rock, it's got . . . everything," he told *MTV News*. "We're just kind of mixingthe pot up and seeing what comes out and trying to put a great record together, just good, positive music. It's a little different, but still the

ABOVE: Kevin makes his Broadway Debut in *Chicago* as lawyer Billy Flynn at the Shubert Theatre on January 20, 2003.

The Boys attend the 2004 Clive Davis Pre-Grammy Party at the iconic Beverly Hills Hotel in Beverly Hills, California.

Emily Kerins poses with the Backstreet Boys elevators at Planet Hollywood in Las Vegas, Nevada.

BACKSTREET ARMY, ASSEMBLE!

The Boys have been a part of my life for as far back as my memories go. They were my first celebrity crushes (still are!) and were my first ever concert. The memory of that first concert will forever be close to my heart. A night when three teenage girls were chauffeured in a limousine to the arena and sang and danced their hearts out to every single song—where they ignored the party poopers behind them when asked to sit down.

At another concert ten years later, the same three girls were upgraded from the nosebleeds to the press box, courtesy of my booted foot and crutches. Best night ever that took us back to childhood. I will forever cherish those memories of a smiling, dancing, laughing friend (who, thank God, loved AJ the most so we didn't have to argue about who would get to marry who) gone too soon.

The Vegas concert was an equally unforgettable experience. The small venue and electric energy made me feel like I was at a private show. Especially when the Boys came into the audience—cannot be outdone! The Backstreet Boys will forever and always be No. 1!

EMILY KERINS ★ KING OF PRUSSIA, PA
KEEPING THE BACKSTREET PRIDE ALIVE SINCE '99

traditional Backstreet sound because you've got all five voices on it."

The Backstreet Boys spent May 2004 attending various summer concerts hosted by radio stations across the US, such as KIIS FM Los Angeles' Wango Tango, Z100 New York City's Zootopia, and Kiss 108 Boston's Kiss Concert. While they were not on the list of performers, they did treat those in attendance to a new song: "Movin' On," a song co-written by Howie. The song originally wasn't a cappella, but they performed it that way at the radio shows and eventually decided to keep the sound. The song would be featured on a tour edition of their next album.

The group also went into the studio with some of their musical heroes that month—Boyz II Men. The legendary R&B vocal group met with the Backstreet Boys in Orlando at Johnny Wright's entertainment compound. Johnny, the man who once helped manage the group, was now their manager again with his company Wright Entertainment Group (WEG), and he also now managed Boyz II Men.

"It was a cool collab," Boyz II Men's Shawn Stockman told the *Orlando Sentinel* in their May 27, 2004, edition. "It felt good, and we want to help one another out."

Unfortunately, the song was never released.

In June 2004, fans stumbled upon a new song on WEG's website. The website included a radio player that played songs from all the artists WEG was managing at that time, and it included an as-yet-unreleased Backstreet Boys song called "Beautiful Woman," which had been recorded for the upcoming album.

ABOVE: The Boys and Avril Lavigne (center) backstage at Madison Square Garden in New York City during Z100's Zootopia 2004.

"Beautiful Woman" would eventually be released on the album.

During that same month, Brian, AJ, and Kevin took part in a charity golf tournament in Franklin, TN, where they and Johnny Wright spoke exclusively about the new music.

"It's not about how many we sell in the first week anymore," AJ told the *Tennessean* in their June 22, 2004, edition. "It's about longevity."

As they continued to work on the album, fans would get to hear more previews. In August 2004, six thirty-second clips of new Backstreet Boys songs were made available by calling various phone numbers by PromoSquad. PromoSquad was a website where music fans could rate new and upcoming songs by artists to generate feedback.

By October 2004, the Boys were nearly done recording the new album, but it would be another eight months before the album would be released.

7
NEVER GONE

....

"Stick the new Backstreet Boys disc in your computer, and you'll see that it shows up in iTunes as a part of the pop category. But don't be fooled. With their first release in nearly five years, the Backstreet Boys have plunged deeply into the adult contemporary pool."

—*Associated Press* review of *Never Gone* ★ June 21, 2005

The Backstreet Boys perform on the German TV show *Wetten, dass..?* in Dresden, Germany, on October 1, 2005.

INCOMPLETE

After performing together for the first time in years at the House of Blues in Orlando, FL, for a hurricane relief concert in September 2004, it was off to Asia for several dates in Japan and China. All five dates in Tokyo, Japan, were sold out. One of the shows even aired on Japanese TV. During these shows, the group performed four new songs that they had recorded for their next album: "Beautiful Woman," "Poster Girl," "Weird World," and "Climbing the Walls."

This was also their first time performing in China. Their Beijing concert was held at the 88,000-seat Beijing Olympic Stadium. A percentage of the proceeds from this concert were donated to Special Olympics International.

Recording for the Boys' next album took them into early 2005. By the time they finished, the Boys had recorded forty-five songs. In addition to Max Martin, they had also worked with producers and writers such as John Ondrasik (Five for Fighting), Dan Muckala, Billy Mann, and Gary Baker, to name a few. Only twelve songs would make the final cut, while other songs would be released as bonus tracks or B-sides on singles. Many of the songs that they had recorded unfortunately leaked online prior to the album's release, reportedly due to AJ losing a CD of the songs at a hotel.

In early February 2005, the music rating websites PromoSquad and Rate the Music had a new Backstreet Boys song for fans to rate. But members of those websites had no idea the song was by the Backstreet Boys, as no artist was listed. Over on the PromoSquad message board, a fan had mentioned the song "Incomplete" was sung by the Backstreet Boys, and members were stunned—and impressed.

Soon after, the song could be heard on radio stations, though it was never officially announced as a new single. Fans would request the song, telling radio stations about it, and DJs would play it. But eventually, radio stations were asked to stop playing the song as the group and label had not officially decided on the new single yet.

"We were narrowing it down to about two or three songs collectively as a group, and we were talking amongst ourselves about it with our management, and the next thing you know, we're getting news that 'Incomplete' is on the radio and on the Internet," AJ said in an interview with MTV on May 27, 2005.

The songs they were deciding between to be the first single were "I Still," "Weird World," and "Incomplete." Despite "Incomplete" not being the first single officially, it generated good feedback amongst fans and radio directors. In the end, the Boys decided to go with "Incomplete" as the first single from their new album.

"'Incomplete' got such a great response from all the program directors and such a great response from the fans that we told them to just go for it," Kevin told MTV.

The single was announced on March 15, 2005, and once it was available for purchase on iTunes, the song went to No. 2 on the iTunes charts. "Incomplete" was released to radio stations on April 4 and quickly became the most requested song on stations such

OPPOSITE: Nick performs live at Z100's Jingle Ball 2005, held at Madison Square Garden in New York City on December 17, 2005.

ABOVE: Nick Carter and AJ McLean greet fans outside their hotel in Oslo, Norway, in October 2005.

as New York's Z100, Los Angeles' KIIS FM, and more. It also became the No. 1 most increased played song on mainstream radio during the same week it was released to radio. More than 115 Top 40 radio stations across the US added the song to their playlists during that week. It was also the No. 1 most-added song on the Top 40.

The song was becoming a success internationally, as well, reaching the Top 10 in fourteen countries. It even peaked at No. 1 in Australia, the Czech Republic, and Hungary. In the US, it would go on to reach No. 13 on the *Billboard* Hot 100 chart, No. 4 on the Digital Song Sales, No. 4 on Adult Contemporary, No. 8 on Mainstream Top 40, and No. 6 on Pop 100 charts. The single was certified gold by the RIAA for sales of 500,000 in the US. On AOL, "Incomplete" was the No. 1 most-played song. AOL even listed the Backstreet Boys as Artist of the Month for the month of June.

The music video for "Incomplete" would be the third video directed by

Joseph Kahn. The video featured the guys in different elements—Brian swimming in the ocean, Nick backed by fire, Howie being showered in the rain, Kevin in snow, and AJ basking in the sun. Joseph Kahn spoke with MTV about the music video shoot and the symbolism in the video.

AJ was represented by the sun because, Kahn said, he's "fiery light and Hollywood cool." Nick was "very volatile at times, beautiful to look at, but dangerous if you get too close," like fire. Howie was the "slick guy in the group," sitting by an old Joshua tree in the video as the wind picked up and a downpour began. Kevin, according to Kahn, was "the most mature and reserved. Colder," thus the snow. Sitting at a white piano, he played the song in a forest as flurries began to fall and smoke rose from the ground. Brian was "this big ball of energy, you can't stop him," and so was represented by the thundering waves of the ocean.

The music video premiered on AOL Music exclusively on April 25, 2005, for twenty-four hours. MTV would premiere the video on April 28, 2005.

THE LAUNCH OF *NEVER GONE*

To gear up for the release of their new album, the Boys set out to tour small clubs in the US, starting on March 21, 2005, in New York City and reaching a total of seventeen cities. Most of the cities on the small tour were on the East Coast, with a few Midwest stops. The group performed twenty songs at each stop on the tour,

Melissa G. poses with Howie Dorough at Planet Hollywood's Miracle Mile Shops in Las Vegas, Nevada, in 2018.

BACKSTREET ARMY, ASSEMBLE!

What do the Backstreet Boys mean to me? Wow . . . that's a loaded question. They mean so many different things and have over the last twenty-eight years. They, at one point, were my escape. When my marriage was rough, they were that fun place I went. When I was struggling . . . they were always there. Now, as an adult, they are my family. They brought me my family. Family isn't always blood. They brought me to places I would have never been. I flew to LA for the first time on my own back in 2012 and haven't looked back. I went on not one but two cruises. I met my best friend, Medina. Friends from all over the world. I am blessed to call Howie and AJ friends. I help moderate the BSB fan club and live out my wildest dreams. So, to me, they mean a whole heck of a lot.

MELISSA G. ★ EDMONTON, AB, CANADA
KEEPING THE BACKSTREET PRIDE ALIVE SINCE '95

The Backstreet Boys performed their first full concert
back together on September 17, 2004. It was a
hurricane benefit concert in Orlando. Brooke Hogan and
Boyz II Men opened for the group, and the Boys performed
never-released songs such as "Climbing the Walls" and
"Poster Girl," which would be on their next album, *Never Gone*.

including five new songs: "Incomplete,"
"I Still," "Weird World," "Poster Girl," and
"Climbing the Walls."

During a stop in Pittsburgh on April 6,
Kevin announced the new album, *Never
Gone*, would be released on June 14, 2005.

Promotion for the new album started
to ramp up, both at home and abroad.
The Backstreet Boys spent most of May
performing at various radio concerts, like
Wango Tango, Zootopia, Kiss 108 Boston,
Y100 Miami's Summer Splash, and others.
They also appeared on shows like *Live with
Regis & Kelly*, *The Today Show*, *TRL*, *The

View*, *The Ellen DeGeneres Show*, *The CBS
Early Show*, and *The Tonight Show with Jay
Leno*. They would also visit Canada, Europe,
and Asia for promotion, appearing at the
MuchMusic Video Awards and on *Musique
Plus*, *Much on Demand*, *TRL UK*, *Top of the
Pops*, *TV Total* (Germany), and had a *Never
Gone* release party in Tokyo. They were
everywhere for the promotion.

While "Incomplete" did well on the radio
and the group worked hard to promote it
around the world, fans struggled to get the
music video onto MTV's *TRL* countdown.
Fans would vote daily, but it barely stayed
on the countdown for eight days. It debuted
at No. 8 on May 3, 2005, and peaked at No.
7 the next day, never getting any higher on
the countdown and never retiring like past
music videos. Fans were frustrated and
started to wonder if MTV no longer cared
about playing the Backstreet Boys.

"It was a top 20 single . . . and fans were
calling into *TRL* requesting our next two
singles," Kevin told *Entertainment Weekly*
in a February 22, 2017, article. "The head
of our music marketing told us, 'MTV said
they're not going to play it. MTV dictates
to the audience what is hip and cool.' That
was disheartening."

Although the video struggled to have
staying power on *TRL*, the video was

BELOW: The Boys
sign *Never Gone*
CDs at the Virgin
Megastore in
Times Square in
New York City in
June 2005.

seemingly doing better online. It was listed at No. 1 on MTV.com's Hot 5 Videos list by May and made the Top 10 of AOL's Most Watched Videos as of June 2005.

Prior to the release of *Never Gone*, fans could listen to the album on-demand in its entirety online. Clear Channel, which owned a majority of the Top 40 radio stations across the US, made the album available across many radio station websites.

The album came with a DVD in some countries that included behind-the-scenes footage of their "Incomplete" music video, a photo gallery, and more. A new format was also released for the album— a DualDisc. One side of the disc was the album in CD format, and the other side was the DVD. This was only released in the US. It included the entire album

in 5.1 Surround Sound on the DVD side, behind the scenes of "Incomplete" and the music video, and a bonus track, "Last Night You Saved My Life."

Never Gone was released on June 14, 2005, and sold over 290,000 copies in the first week in the US, debuting at No. 3 on the *Billboard* 200 chart. This was their fifth consecutive release to reach the Top 10 on *Billboard*. The album charted in the Top 10 in seventeen countries and reached No. 1 in Germany and Greece. The album also went platinum in the US for having sold over 1.7 million copies. In Australia, it was certified platinum for sales of 70,000. In Canada, 100,000 copies were sold, and in Japan, it was certified two-times platinum for sales of 500,000. As of July 2007, the album had sold three million copies worldwide.

ABOVE: The Boys perform at Hartwall Arena in Helsinki, Finland, in October 2005.

HB0917E GENADM10211008
K-HFAN
HB0917E
61.00
GENERAL ADMISSN 61.00
HOB & XL 106.7 PRESENT
10.40
BACKSTREET BOYS
GENADM
W/SPEC GUEST BOYZ II MEN
HOB-ORL/GEN ADM STANDING
NO CAMERAS/ALL AGES
FRI SEP 17 2004 DRS@ 7PM
CN 11642
GENADM
CA600HOB
1021
61.00
1008
NO REFUNDS
NO EXCHANGES
HOUSE OF BLUES

ABOVE: The Backstreet Boys perform their first full concert since 2001 at the House of Blues in Orlando for a hurricane benefit concert on September 17, 2004.

While sales were down compared to previous albums, partly due to illegal downloading, the Backstreet Boys still managed solid numbers, especially considering they had not released a new album in almost five years. Critics had mixed reviews of the album, with outlets like E! Online and *Entertainment Weekly* rating the album a C, *Rolling Stone* giving it a one-star rating, and others like *Blender* giving a two-star rating. *USA Today* and *All Music* gave the album three stars.

Fans also had mixed feelings about the album. Many enjoyed this new sound and wanted the group to continue in this direction, while others preferred a more R&B/pop sound, similar to the tracks that the Boys had recorded earlier. *Never Gone* was an album that was heavily debated amongst fans on message boards years after the release.

The second single was "Just Want You to Know," another Max Martin-written track. This song was more pop/rock sounding than "Incomplete." For the music video, the Boys were a fictional hair band from the 1980s called Sphynkter. They also appeared as fans of the band. An alternate video—mostly showing the

Boys performing as the hair band—was also released on the *Never Gone: The Video* DVD and a tour edition of the album released in certain countries, which also included a DVD with their videos.

The Never Gone Tour began July 22, 2005, in West Palm Beach, FL, and ended on February 2, 2006, in Melbourne, Australia. The setlist included twenty-one songs, including six songs from *Never Gone*.

The third and final single off *Never Gone* varied, depending on your location. In Europe and other countries around the world, the single was "I Still." In the US, it was "Crawling Back to You," a song released on October 11, 2005, in support of "Music For Hurricane Relief." The song only managed to reach No. 30 on the *Billboard* Adult Contemporary, No. 31 on the Mainstream Top 40, and No. 51 on the Pop 100. No music video was filmed for the song.

"I Still" was released on November 25, 2005, and it didn't have the same success as other singles. While it peaked at No. 8 on the Dutch Top 40 Tipparade, it only managed to reach No. 45 in Germany; in most countries, it only peaked in the top 100.

BACKSTREET BECOMES FOUR

A new era and a new change were coming to the group. For months in 2005 and 2006, there were rumors among fans that Kevin was planning to leave the group. Fans didn't want to believe it.

BELOW: The Boys during the Recording Academy Honors 2006 at Loews Miami Beach Hotel in Miami, Florida.

ABOVE: The Boys were the musical guest on *The Tonight Show with Jay Leno* on November 2, 2007.

On April 17, 2006, the group was honored at the Recording Academy Honors, to mark their success in the music industry to that point. It would be the last time all five members would appear in public together for many years.

On June 24, 2006, Kevin's departure was confirmed on the Backstreet Boys' official website, just as the guys were set to go back in the studio to work on a new album.

"Earlier this year, after much soul-searching, Kevin Richardson came to us and told us that he had decided to leave the group and pursue other interests. He gave his blessing to continue the music without him.

"We have no intention of replacing Kevin, and the door will always be open for him to return to the Backstreet Boys. We wish him all the best in his future endeavors." A statement by Kevin was made on the group's official website, as well:

After thirteen years of what can only be described as a dream come true, I have decided that it is time to leave the Backstreet Boys. It was a very tough decision for me, but one that was necessary in order to move on with the next chapter of my life. Howard, Brian, Alex, and Nick will always be my little brothers and have my utmost love and support. I would like to thank the Backstreet fans for all the beautiful memories we have shared together, and look forward to including you in the next phase of my life. I wish my brothers continued success and look forward to their new album.

Many fans were surprised by Kevin's departure; some even stepped away as fans during that time.

"My immediate reaction to Kevin leaving was disappointment, but not because of the fact he left. It was because of *how* the group announced he left," Gemma from Canada said. "Throughout the Boys' entire career up until this point, when big stuff went down, like Brian's heart surgery or AJ going to rehab, the group would always go on a TV show or record a video statement in person addressing these massive things that I felt affected me. The day Kevin leaving was announced, I went on the group's website like I would every day, and it was just there like any other news update. After that? Nothing. He was just gone, and the group was four guys."

Kim Schussler was also concerned.

"I definitely was selfishly upset because I thought it was the end of the group as we all knew it forever. I was hopeful when they announced they were continuing as a foursome, but just had this fear that they'd eventually fade away and I wouldn't see or hear them again."

Many bands say that they will continue when a member leaves, and some do. Duran Duran continued when both Andy Taylor and Roger Taylor left. New Kids on the Block tried to continue and did for a short time after Jonathan Knight left the band. And let's not talk about the revolving door of members of New Edition.

Though Nick, AJ, Brian, and Howie said that they would continue to be the Backstreet Boys, there was always that little part in the back of fans' minds that wondered if it would work.

It was certainly an emotional time for everyone in the Boys' universe.

BELOW: The Boys visit TRL at MTV Studios Times Square on October 30, 2007 in New York City.

8
IN PIECES

"The vocals remain solid, the harmonies smooth. Familiar and safe, there's nothing extraordinary about 'Unbreakable,' but at the same time, it's completely inoffensive. But you have to give the Backstreet Boys credit for this much: ten years after the heyday of their genre, they've found a way to remain productive, if not entirely relevant."

—Christy Lemire ★ *Associated Press*, November 23, 2007

AJ, Nick, Howie, and Brian sign autographs at the New Yorker Hotel in Cologne, Germany, in 2007.

UNBREAKABLE

Replacing Kevin Richardson was never an option for the Backstreet Boys.

After Kevin left the group, the remaining four guys had offers for a reality TV show where they would pick Kevin's replacement. According to reports, the group also turned down the chance to change the group's name to just "Backstreet."

"I really think he's going to miss it. I really do," AJ told *Billboard Magazine* in an article from October 12, 2007. "Some of the other guys you could ask, and they'd probably tell you the total opposite. Me, I really believe he may come back."

After taking time to digest Kevin's departure, Nick, Howie, Brian, and AJ went into the studio for the first time without him. While they were planning out the album, Nick was in Los Angeles filming a reality show with his siblings, *House of Carters*. A meeting with the Boys' management and a recording session was included in the show, which aired in the fall of 2006 on E!.

In January 2007, the Backstreet Boys went on a writing trip to Nashville, TN, for six weeks to work with producer and songwriter Dan Muckala. In addition to Kevin's absence, this would also be the first album created without longtime producer and writer Max Martin.

"We've been together for fifteen years. We're like family," Howie told the *Morning Star* in its November 15, 2007, edition, of recording their new album without Kevin.

RIGHT: A photo from the press room at Z100's Jingle Ball 2007.

"To me, it almost feels like the first son going off to college, but the rest of the family household still keeps moving on."

The group spent most of August 2007 promoting the first single, "Inconsolable," and the forthcoming album, *Unbreakable*, on various radio stations across the US. The group was divided into two groups to reach more radio stations: Nick with Howie and AJ with Brian.

The group visited New York City radio station Z100 to premiere "Inconsolable" on August 6, 2007. The song was written and produced by Emanuel Kiriakou and co-written by Lindy Robbins and Jess Cates.

Despite visiting various radio stations across the US, the song didn't make much of an impact. It only peaked at No. 86 on the *Billboard* Hot 100, although it fared better on the Adult Contemporary chart, peaking at No. 21. The highest chart position came from Italy, where the song peaked at No. 2. On Mediabase, a radio airplay tracking website, the song only had 1382 spins on Top 40 mainstream radio by October 4, 2007.

Meanwhile, music rating websites PromoSquad and Rate the Music had a few clips of the songs "Unmistakable" and "Something That I Already Know" available for music fans to rate.

ABOVE: The Boys onstage at Z100's Jingle Ball 2007 at Madison Square Garden in New York.

Unbreakable was released on October 30, 2007, in the US. The album had been released a week earlier, on October 24, 2007, in Japan. Due to this, the album was leaked online, allowing it to be downloaded illegally. While album sales continued to decline overall in the music industry, the album still managed to reach the Top 10 on the *Billboard* 200 chart at No. 7. It sold 81,123 copies in the first week in the US. In Japan, the album reached No. 1 on the Oricon chart and was certified platinum for sales of 250,000. Over in Canada, the album debuted at No. 2 on the *Billboard* Canadian Albums chart and was certified gold for sales of 50,000.

Nick, Brian, Howie, and AJ had writing credits on four songs. What was interesting to see was that former *NSYNC member, JC Chasez, had co-written a song with AJ called "Treat Me Right" for the album. This was the first time the Backstreet Boys would have a song written by a former member of a "rival" boy band.

The second and final single off *Unbreakable* was a ballad called "Helpless When She Smiles." Most may not know this, but the song had actually been recorded by another artist prior to the Boys recording it: Bastiaan Ragas, a former member of the boy band Caught in the Act, in 2005. The song was also released by country singer Michael Dean Church in 2008.

"Helpless When She Smiles" failed to make an impact on radio and on the charts. It never charted on the *Billboard* Hot 100 or on any other chart in the US. It did, however, peak at No. 4 in Italy and at No. 34 in Germany.

Along with the new album came a new beginning. In December 2008, Howie married his longtime girlfriend, Leigh, in Orlando, in a Catholic ceremony at St. James Cathedral. The couple had met in 2000 when the Backstreet Boys increased their web presence and online fan club, and Leigh, a former film exec and real estate broker, was hired to help with the effort.

ON THE ROAD AGAIN

The Backstreet Boys began their *Unbreakable* world tour on February 16 in Tokyo, Japan, and it ran until March 13, 2009, ending in Puebla, Mexico. The setlist included twenty-seven to twenty-eight songs. Initially, nine of the songs were from *Unbreakable*, though some would either be replaced or removed. The Boys each did a solo performance too. Nick sang a medley of "I Got You" and "Blow Your Mind" from his album *Now or Never*; he later opted to only perform "I Got You." Brian sang "Welcome Home (You)" from his Christian album, *Welcome Home*. AJ sang an unreleased song, "Drive By Love," and Howie sang "She's Like The Sun," another unreleased track that Howie had recorded for a solo album.

Andie Yammine poses with the Backstreet Boys during the 2019 DNA World Tour.

BACKSTREET ARMY, ASSEMBLE!

Backstreet Boys have been together for twenty-nine years as of this writing (reaching year thirty by the time this book is published), and I've been a fan for twenty-seven of those years. I was one of the lucky people in Canada who was given first access to the Boys. A radio programmer from Montreal (my hometown) was one of the first people to introduce them to our airwaves. My love for the band was instantaneous. My favorite member of the band, Kevin, has always been my favorite and has proven to be a great source of inspiration in my life. I respect him and the other boys on so many levels.

While I was never able to see the band live as a kid, adult me has had the pleasure of seeing and meeting them quite often. The feelings that I felt as a youngster have only intensified as I watch BSB perform as an adult. Maybe they've become more talented, or maybe I just appreciate them more now? They are stellar performers, and you can tell that they still enjoy being on stage/interacting with us. I hope that never changes.

For the band who has been with me for all these years, thank you for always giving your all, and here's to the next thirty!

ANDIE YAMMINE ★ CALGARY, AB, CANADA
KEEPING THE BACKSTREET PRIDE ALIVE SINCE '95

ABOVE: Howie, Brian, Nick, and AJ perform on MTV's *Total Finale Live*, the last episode of *TRL*, at MTV studios on October 28, 2008 in New York City.

While in Europe and Asia, the Boys were still able to perform in arenas such as the O2 in London; in the US and Canada, things were scaled back some. They were playing in theaters, small arenas, and amphitheaters with a seating capacity that varied between two thousand to over thirteen thousand.

Their London show was filmed for Control Room and MSN's "Music in Concert," an online platform where you could watch concerts of various artists. The concert was made available on June 26, 2008. Fans in the UK had the opportunity to relive the concert when it aired on VH1 on October 31, 2008. The concert also aired on HDnet in the US on February 15, 2009. Solo performances during the show were

cut from the online version and TV airings of the show.

While on the *Unbreakable* tour with the Backstreet Boys in Europe, Nick began noticing chest pain and extreme fatigue, something he had never really experienced before. Nick went to a doctor, where he was diagnosed with cardiomyopathy, a weakening of the heart muscle caused by years of abusing his body with drugs and alcohol. Cardiomyopathy took the lives of actor Chris Penn, who was only forty at the time of his death, and thirty-year-old singer Andy Gibb.

"I don't want to die," Carter told *People* in their February 5, 2009 edition. "I don't want to be that person people read about and think, 'That's sad that he couldn't stop it and killed himself."

Nick credits a book that Kevin gave him when he was twenty-one, *Why Some Positive Thinkers Get Powerful Results,* by Norman Vincent Peale, with helping him turn his life around, as well as moving to the Nashville, Tennessee, area and leaving the Hollywood scene behind.

THIS IS US

"Straight Through My Heart," the first single from the group's upcoming seventh studio album, was released on August 27, 2009. The up-tempo dance track was produced by acclaimed producer RedOne, known then for his work with Lady Gaga.

The song never charted on the main *Billboard* charts in the United States,

although it did hit No. 6 on *Billboard*'s Bubbling Under Hot 100 and No. 18 on the *Billboard* Hot Dance Club Songs. It was a Top 5 hit in Japan, Mexico, South Korea, and Scotland, and a Top 10 hit in Sweden.

The music video, directed by Kai Regan, had the Backstreet Boys take on the persona of "Day Walkers," who help and protect humans from vampires at clubs and bars.

The Backstreet Boys released their seventh studio album, the second without Kevin, on October 6, 2009. The album, *This Is Us,* brought the group back to their R&B/pop roots, working with Ne-Yo, Pitbull, T-Pain, Ryan Tedder, Claude Kelly, Jim Jonsin, and RedOne, along with Max Martin, Rami Yacoub, and Kristian Lundin.

"We really wanted to push the envelope with this record," Howie told the *Pittsburgh Post-Gazette* in their August 23, 2010, edition. "We wanted to reach out to some

BELOW: AJ, Nick, Howie, and Brian appear on the German TV show *Guinness World Records* in Cologne, Germany, on November 23, 2007.

RIGHT: The Backstreet Boys perform at a radio station Halloween concert in Charlotte, North Carolina, on October 14, 2009.

BELOW: Nick performs during a special acoustic concert the Backstreet Boys held in Miami, Florida, on December 8, 2010, the night before their first cruise.

OPPOSITE: Brian performs in Valdosta, Georgia, on June 5, 2010, during the This Is Us Tour.

writers that people wouldn't have expected us to reach out to."

However, before the album was released, fans got to listen to some of the new songs due to yet another leak on the internet. It was later revealed that a hacker known as DJ Stolen was the culprit, and that they had placed music by Mariah Carey, Lady Gaga, Leona Lewis, Usher, and others online early, as well. The Backstreet Boys were angry about the leak but gained a little insight into what fans thought.

"It was interesting because we got to see which songs were more popular than others," AJ told DigitalSpy.com on July 27, 2009. "The ones we thought were better weren't necessarily the ones the fans liked—it was a fifty-fifty thing, which is good."

While in New York City, gearing up for the release of *This Is Us* with the usual promotion, Brian was diagnosed with swine flu, a respiratory infection. Appearances at

the Hard Rock Café and on CBS' *The Early Show* were canceled.

Even without a lot of promotion, *This Is Us* debuted at No. 9 on the *Billboard* 200

chart, making them the first group to have its first seven charted albums in the Top 10 since Sade. The next week the album dropped to No. 64 and was only on the chart for five weeks. The album peaked at No. 2 in Japan, No. 3 in Canada, and No. 10 in Germany.

While sales were low, even with the digitally-charged atmosphere of the music business, *This Is Us* received good reviews.

"Although the lyrics never reach too far, the foursome simmers because the album's production keeps the singers' harmonizing," Jason Lipshutz from *Billboard* said in the October 3, 2009, edition. "'This Is Us' may be a steppingstone in ushering Backstreet Boys away from their days on pop radio and firmly through the club door."

After a few radio station appearances, such as one in Charlotte, North Carolina, at a Halloween concert, the Backstreet Boys hit the road for their *This Is Us* tour with their first stop in Lisbon, Portugal, on October 30, 2009. The tour was a lot simpler than their previous tours. The group was joined by four female dancers who performed alongside them or joined them for skits on stage. When the group took a break to change outfits, each member had a movie-themed skit that played on a huge screen onstage. AJ became a character in *Fight Club*, Nick in *The Matrix*, Howie in *The Fast and the Furious*, and Brian in *Enchanted*.

The tour had fairly favorable reviews from journalists. "The production values and visual candy have been stripped down since the Backstreet Boys concerts of yore," Amanda Ash of the *Vancouver Sun* said in the August 7, 2010, edition. "They threw out the excessive pyrotechnics and

Jessica Moffett and her best friend, Lisa, pose with the Backstreet Boys during their In A World Like This Tour.

BACKSTREET ARMY, ASSEMBLE!

My best friend, Lisa, and I have been die-hard Backstreet Boys fans since 1998. Our mutual love of their music has been an anchor of our friendship. We have been to eleven concerts, twice during their Las Vegas residency, but my favorite BSB experience was when we got to meet them during the In A World Like This Tour. They were sweet and gracious, everything you want when meeting your idols. We even made them laugh when we asked to switch positions in the group photo so that we could stand next to our favorites, Lisa next to Nick and me next to Brian. I'm forever grateful for the Backstreet Boys and all the joy they've brought me in my life. KTBSPA.

JESSICA MOFFETT ★ CONSHOHOCKEN, PA
KEEPING THE BACKSTREET PRIDE ALIVE SINCE '98

intricate choreography for toned-down dance numbers and a more mature, music-centric approach."

BYE, BYE, JIVE

On May 27, 2010, just before the *This Is Us* tour began in the United States, the Backstreet Boys announced that they were leaving their long-time label, Jive Records.

In a post on the official site called "Freedom: Backstreet Boys," the group made a short but sweet statement about leaving Jive: "So the news is out! The Backstreet Boys are no longer signed to long-time record label Jive Records. The amicable split is very exciting for the group."

"This is the best thing, at the best time that could have ever happened for us," Brian said in the post. "We are confident in the future of our band and are looking forward to the new things to come. 2011 is going to be a great year for us! KTBSPA!"

The group has never really gone into great detail about the split, but the label did not last long after the group left. While Jive/BMG was bought by Sony Music Entertainment in 2008, it remained a label until Jive was merged with RCA Records in 2011.

"HANGIN' TOUGH"

At the same time, the Backstreet Boys were on their *This Is Us* tour, and New Kids on the Block were on their Casi-NO Tour. Part of the New Kids on the Block show included performing part of "I Want It That Way." To the surprise of fans at the show in New York's Radio City Music Hall, Nick, AJ, Brian, and Howie joined the New Kids onstage for the song. After that surprise performance, rumors began circulating that the group would do a joint tour the next year. Members of both groups teased the collaboration before an official announcement was made.

On November 10, 2010, on *On Air with Ryan Seacrest*, it was formally announced that not only were the Backstreet Boys and New Kids on the Block recording a new song together, but the group would release a full album and tour in the summer of 2011. The NKOTBSB tour was originally supposed to be twelve dates but expanded to twenty-four and then fifty-one, hitting cities such as Atlanta, Orlando, Chicago, and Los Angeles.

To promote the upcoming tour, the newly formed mega-group, NKOTBSB, performed a medley of their hit songs at the 38th Annual American Music Awards later that month, causing artists such as Ke$ha and

AJ became the fourth Backstreet Boy to tie the knot when he married make-up artist Rochelle Karidis on December 11, 2011, at the Beverly Hills Hotel. Instead of being traditional, the wedding had a goth theme, where Rochelle wore a black wedding dress and walked down the aisle to Guns N' Roses' "November Rain."

ABOVE: Brian, Howie, Nick, and AJ attend the 2009 MTV European Music Awards in Berlin, Germany, on November 5, 2009.

Pat Monahan of Train to dance and sing along. After the awards performance, NKOTBSB were asked to perform live in Times Square for *Dick Clark's New Year's Rockin' Eve* on ABC, where they again performed medleys of their biggest hits, such as "Please Don't Go Girl," "I Want It That Way," "Everybody," and "Hangin' Tough."

NKOTBSB, the album, was released on May 24, 2011, coinciding with the start of the tour the next day in Chicago, IL. The album featured five of the Backstreet Boys' biggest hits and five of New Kids on the Block's biggest hits, plus three extra songs—"Don't Turn Out The Lights," "All In My Head," and an NKOTBSB mash-up.

"Don't Turn Out the Lights" became the only single from the album. It was written by frequent Backstreet Boys collaborators Emanuel Kiriakou, Jess Cates, and Claude Kelly. While the song peaked at No. 46 in Canada, it debuted at No. 14 on the US *Billboard* Bubbling Under Hot 100 singles. The second song, "All in My Head," was originally an unreleased Backstreet Boys track that had been recorded for their previous album, *This Is Us*. The third song, the mash-up, was six and a half minutes long and featured both groups' biggest hits.

"But from the start, NKOTB and BSB came out to entertain, and the audience didn't leave disappointed," Kimberly Nordyke of the *Hollywood Reporter* said in a July 2, 2011, review of the tour. "Sure, the costumes may be less flashy, the hair a little thinner, and the voices a bit lower—the Kids and the Boys are now their thirties and forties—but inside Staples Center, fans were transported back in time. The groups knew what the fans wanted—hit songs, flashes of skin, and some well-choreographed dance moves—and they more than delivered."

During the Los Angeles show at the Staples Center, Backstreet Boys fans were surprised when former member Kevin Richardson came out on stage to perform his bridge of "I Want It That Way."

"Wow, this feels good," Kevin told the crowd after the song. It wouldn't be the last time Backstreet Boys fans saw him that year.

The NKOTBSB tour ran through August to accommodate New Kid Donnie Wahlberg's filming schedule on his hit TV show, *Blue Bloods*. At the end of 2011, the NKOTBSB tour was ranked eighth on *Billboard*'s Top 25 Tours, earning more than $76 million.

ROLL MY WINDOWS DOWN AND CRUISE

In December 2010, the Backstreet Boys had taken to the seas for their very first cruise, called "SS Backstreet." At that time, fans took up half of the Carnival cruise ship. In 2011, it was a full charter—a cruise ship *full* of Backstreet Boys fans.

BELOW: The Boys on tour to promote their *This Is Us* album in 2010.

New Kids On The Block and the Backstreet Boys perform together for their NKOTBSB Tour at the US Airways Center in Phoenix, Arizona, on July 1, 2011.

The 2011 cruise left from Miami on December 2 and would return on December 5. It included a stop for a beach party in Nassau, Bahamas, and featured deck parties each night with themes, such as a Sphynkter night for fans to dress up in '80s gear as the Boys donned their hair band costumes from their "Just Want You To Know" music video. There were also activities, such as karaoke, a concert, and a game show.

Fans got a surprise on the second day of the cruise when they disembarked and headed toward a hotel resort in Nassau for the beach party: Kevin Richardson. Kevin joined the Boys for a day of games on the beach, and the five of them performed an a cappella snippet of "Safest Place to Hide" for the crowd. That night for the concert, Kevin joined the Boys on stage

on the boat to perform "Drowning" and also took part in that night's deck party theme—Prom Night.

At one point in the evening, Kevin was standing on the balcony, overlooking the lido deck, and watching fans as they danced and had fun in their prom dresses. He had tears in his eyes. He missed being a Backstreet Boy.

GUESS WHO'S BACK, BACK AGAIN?

NKOTBSB went back on tour in 2012, but this time they were off to Europe with the same show that had toured North America the year before. The tour started in Ireland before making its way to England, where the

BELOW LEFT: AJ celebrates the 2011 Backstreet Boys Cruise setting sail.

BELOW RIGHT: Nick performs as a member of Sphynkter on the 2011 cruise.

supergroup performed two nights in a row at London's O2 Arena. The first night was more like a dress rehearsal since the next night would be streamed live in movie theatres and on the internet for millions to see.

"I think we should let them in on a secret we have," Nick told Brian on stage during the show. "Since we love you guys so much, especially London, that we are going to come back in July to record the next Backstreet Boys album this year."

"Wait, there's two parts to that secret. You told them the first part," Brian added. "Should I tell them the second part?"

Fans cheered as Nick asked if he was going to tell it right there.

"And Kevin is coming back!" Brian exclaimed. The crowd went wild.

What fans had speculated for months was now official—Kevin Richardson would be coming back to the Backstreet Boys, and the group would be whole again.

But there was more big news to be shared.

During a break in the show, when both New Kids on the Block and Backstreet Boys would introduce the band and talk about what it was like to tour together, AJ announced he had news to share. He took off his shirt and vest to show he had on a sleeveless shirt underneath. He turned around to show off a bedazzled DADDY TO BE. He and his new wife, Rochelle, were expecting their first child.

The Backstreet Boys were about to enter a new era in their lives and career. Kevin was coming back, and a third, the fourth Backstreet Boy was about to become a father. Plus, a new album was coming, without Jive Records looking over their shoulder and dictating the songs and collaborators.

BELOW (LEFT AND RIGHT): Kevin Richardson surprises cruise guests by attending the beach party on the 2011 Backstreet Boys cruise.

SHOW 'EM (WHAT YOU'RE MADE OF)

"Superb, often spine-tingling harmonies—always Backstreet Boys' chief strength—abound, be it in the multi-layered standout 'Soldier' or the breezy title track, which even carries hints of Tom Petty at his most windswept."

—John Zilewood ★ *Evening Standard*, July 26, 2013

Amongst the stars: On April 22, 2013, the Boys celebrated their twenty-year career with a ceremony honoring them with a star on the Hollywood Walk of Fame.

ABOVE: The Backstreet Boys performed live at the *Good Morning America* Summer Concert Series on August 31, 2012.

LET THE WORK BEGIN

After the NKOTBSB tour ended, Nick, AJ, Brian, and Howie had a small break before they headed to London in July with Kevin to begin work on new material. The group moved into a small house, all together, for the first time in a long time. In fact, it was the first time the guys had lived together since the older members of the group lived together during the early days of the group. And to make it better, cameras were there to capture it all for a documentary that the group had decided to film while recording this first album back together with all five members.

But the writing for the album didn't start there. Back in April 2012, before the announcement that Kevin would be coming back to the group, all five members had met with producer Martin Terefe in London to write songs for the new album.

The group got back to work on the album on July 9, 2012, tweeting out, "First day in London working on our next album has already been amazing. So much great new music out here. This is going to be fun!"

On July 17, 2012, the Backstreet Boys went live on ABC's *Good Morning America* from the studio to discuss working on the new album and to announce that they would perform for the first time since Kevin came back at a show on August 31 in New York.

"It's awesome, it really is. The vibe is fantastic," Nick told *Good Morning America*. "It's just been really organic. Our vibe is like never before. It's revitalized."

Besides Martin Tarefe, the guys also worked with Sacha Skarbek, known later for Miley Cyrus' "Wrecking Ball," and British singer/songwriter Craig David while in London. Back in the United States, the Backstreet Boys worked with Morgan Reid, Mika Guillory, Lucas Hilbert, Geo Slam, GoodWill & MGI, and Porcelain Black.

Most importantly, Nick, AJ, Brian, Kevin, and Howie were writing their own songs on the new album, which was important to them.

"We all discussed, we want this to be a personal record," Kevin told *MTV News* on July 9, 2012. "We want it to be authentic to us and who we are and where we're at in our lives."

After the guys began recording, Brian had something important to tell the band—something they may have already noticed. Something was up with the angelic voice he was known for.

According to an interview with the *Huffington Post*, AJ said that Brian sat the group down to tell him about his vocal disorder—vocal (muscle) tension dysphonia (MTD).

According to the Department of Otolaryngology at the University of Pittsburgh, muscle tension dysphonia is an "imbalance in the coordination of the muscles and breathing patterns needed to create voice." The most common symptom is a "change in voice quality, ranging from

LEFT: AJ performs during the In A World Like This Tour at Jones Beach, New York, on August 13, 2013.

mild to severe and is often associated with pain or discomfort when speaking."

In Brian's case, sometimes his voice would crack or just not come out. Fans had begun noticing the changes in his voice during the NKOTBSB tour.

"It comes from stress," Brian told Annie Reuter of CBS Radio. "It comes from being tense. It comes from overuse, overwork. We've had a lot of singing parts to sing over the years. I'm not eighteen anymore."

"It's a tough struggle for me to be what people expect me to be," he added.

IT'S CHRISTMAS TIME AGAIN

While still working on their new album, the Backstreet Boys were approached by Disney to perform in their *Disney Parks Christmas Day Parade* for Christmas 2012. The network asked if they wanted to perform "Christmas Time," a song that they had released in December 1996, or a Christmas classic.
The Boys had another idea.

While already working with Morgan Taylor Reid and Mika Guillory, Nick and Howie began writing a Christmas song. According to an interview with Tommy2.net in November 2012, Howie said that it took two hours to write the song. Within a week, "It's Christmas Time Again" had been demoed, and the other Backstreet Boys had recorded their parts. Disney loved it and approved it for the television special.

"You know, it came together really effortlessly, and you know, it's something

that I feel like it's definitely current, hip, modern. It's almost like a Backstreet Boys meet Coldplay kind of vibe, and it's just something that not only are our fans really enjoying, but a lot of people who are not normally Backstreet Boys fans have come up to me and said, 'Wow, this song is really great.' So, it's awesome," Howie told Tommy2.net.

The song received positive reviews and peaked at No. 1 on the *Billboard* US Holiday Digital Songs chart in November 2012 and No. 38 on the Japan Hot 100.

TWENTY YEARS

On March 1, 2013, it was announced on the Backstreet Boys website that the Boys would be receiving a star on the Hollywood Walk of Fame. In that same announcement, they let fans know that they would be celebrating their upcoming twentieth anniversary with an event but hadn't revealed any details yet. They later held a contest through the official fan club to win entry into the anniversary event.

The Backstreet Boys celebrated twenty years together with a huge celebration in Los Angeles on April 20, 2013: Live from Hollywood: Backstreet Boys Celebration of Twenty Years. The event was held at the Fonda Theater and was also livestreamed (for a fee of $6.99) by iGO HD for fans who could not attend. JoJo Wright from KIIS FM Los Angeles and singer Tamee Harrison hosted, giving a behind-the-scenes look at the festivities, as well as interacting with fans watching the livestream and giving away prizes to those who correctly

Nicole and Kevin at the Kentucky Music Hall of Fame 2015 Induction Ceremony in Lexington, Kentucky.

BACKSTREET ARMY, ASSEMBLE!

Kevin means the world to me. I love and adore him. Kevin's voice always brings joy to my life. It's healing and has gotten me through so many things. He has a natural talent—style and grace. He is an amazing entertainer. His swag is unbelievable.

I was extremely sad when he took a break from the group but understood why he did it. It was an admirable move he made for personal reasons, and I respect him for that. Words can't describe how elated I was when he decided to return.

He inspires his fans and makes them feel special and appreciated. I appreciate the time he took to message me when my dad passed away. It was unexpected, and I'll never forget that he did that for me. His positivity is admirable.

The humility Kevin possesses is incredible. I'm thankful that I have been given the opportunity to come and see him perform and for the times I was able to meet him in person. I'm thankful that he is continuously making my Backstreet dreams come true. He is my favorite person in the world (after my mom), my happy place, and I'm proud to be a fan.

NICOLE M. ★ TORONTO, ON, CANADA
KEEPING THE BACKSTREET PRIDE ALIVE SINCE '96

answered trivia questions about the group. They also interviewed fans at the event and had them sing Backstreet Boys songs.

During the event, a video was shown with messages from fans and celebrities congratulating the Boys on twenty years. The celebrities included New Kids on The Block, Kathy Griffin, Niall Horan, Fifth Harmony, Perez Hilton, and The Wanted.

The Boys talked about the past twenty years, their current plans, and fan encounters, and also previewed music from their album *In A World Like This* and discussed the songs. A ten-minute clip of their documentary, *Show 'Em What You're Made Of*, was also shown for the fans at the event only. During the livestream, JoJo spoke with Howie and Nick about the documentary and the group's visits to each of their hometowns. The documentary had allowed them to get to know more things about each other than they'd known before. Later, the Boys answered questions from fans watching at home (who submitted them on Twitter) and those who were in attendance. Once the event ended, fans lined up to meet the Boys and get a photo taken.

A few days later, on April 22, 2013, the Backstreet Boys were presented with a star on the Hollywood Walk of Fame.

The Boys were there with families, friends, and thousands of fans, who had lined up early in the morning to watch the unveiling of the star. The star was placed near Live Nation's building at 7072 Hollywood Boulevard. Also in attendance was Max Martin, who gave a speech about the Boys:

I met these guys in Sweden, Stockholm, in the mid-nineties. They were coming out to record with my mentor and friend, Denniz PoP. I didn't know much about them. I've seen some clips on some VHS, something like that. So, we took them out to dinner, and I told them, so I'm excited to hear you sing finally in the studio later tonight. "We'll perform right now." So, they stand up in this kind of hipster place restaurant with caps, backpacks, and they sing for the place. "I'll Never Break Your Heart." And I got the goosebumps. It was amazing. And a lot of things changed after that night for me. We got to go along with you on a ride around the world. Amazing ride of music. A lot of things have changed. You now have babies. You're married. Some things haven't changed. You look the same. It's actually amazing—not that, you know, weird in this part of the world, but still worth mentioning and another thing that hasn't changed. We were in the studio a few weeks ago

recording a song, and when these guys started singing, I still got the goosebumps. They're simply amazing. So, when I got the question to come here to speak today, I felt that this was one more moment my opportunity to say thank you to you guys because you changed my life, and I'm going to use an Abba quote. I can do that because I'm Swedish, and Swedes can do that whenever they want, you know. Thank you for the music.

ABOVE: On April 22, 2013, the Boys received the 2,495th star in the category of Recording on the Walk of Fame on Hollywood Boulevard, near the Live Nation Building.

IN A WORLD LIKE THIS

Before releasing the first single from the upcoming album, the Backstreet Boys released a song called "Permanent Stain" on May 20, 2013. They had performed the upbeat song a few days earlier for the first time on *Good Morning America*. The song came free when you purchased tickets to their upcoming *In A World Like This* US tour, which was set to begin in August.

"Permanent Stain," co-written by Nick, was just a tease for fans of what was coming with their new music. Thankfully, fans would not have to wait long to hear even more.

The Backstreet Boys' lead single from their upcoming eighth studio album, *In A World Like This*, was released digitally on

RIGHT: The Backstreet Boys rehearse during soundcheck before their In A World Like This Tour in Holmdel Township, New Jersey, on August 15, 2013.

BELOW: Baylee Littrell and Mason Richardson join the Boys on stage.

June 25, 2013. The song, which the new album would be named after, was written by longtime friend and collaborator Max Martin, along with Kristian Lundin and Savan Kotecha. The song was one of the last that they recorded for the new album after the Boys got word that their old partner had a song for them.

The fact that the Backstreet Boys and Max Martin, who was now a hitmaker for Kelly Clarkson, Taylor Swift, Pink, and more, were working together was a big deal, not only for fans but for the Boys themselves.

"We've changed each other's lives," Nick Carter told MTV on May 16, 2013. "Everything seems right now. It just seems like the right fit. The right time for him because he's a really busy man, but what we created together from our hits . . . they're kind of like masterpieces in his mind. So, he wanted to live up to that in a certain way. So that's why it took this long to maybe come back around. It was just the right time for both of us."

While the single did not enter the US *Billboard* Charts, it did reach No. 18 on the Hot Single Sales chart. The single went gold in Japan, reaching No. 6 on the Oricon Singles Chart, No. 1 on the Adult Contemporary Chart, and No. 3 on the Airplay Chart. "In A World Like This" also topped the charts for four weeks in China.

Just a month later, on July 30, 2013, the entire album was released.

In A World Like This was the Backstreet Boys' first album not put out by Jive Records. They released it through their own K-BAHN record label (made up of their initials) and under license through BMG Rights Management, with distribution through RED distribution.

The album was released five days earlier in Japan and debuted at No. 1 on the charts there. In the United States, the album became the group's highest-charting album since *Never Gone* in 2005, when it debuted at No. 5 on the US *Billboard* 200 chart. On the Independent Albums Chart and the Digital Albums Chart, the album debuted at No. 1. The album went No. 1 in China, Switzerland, and the Netherlands, and on the Japan International Charts. It was also a Top 5 hit in Spain, Germany, and Canada and Top 10 in Norway and Australia.

Critics gave mixed reviews of the album, with some loving the change in direction and others enjoying their previous album, *This Is Us*, more.

"'In A World Like This' is a well-crafted executive of solid material, more genuine and endearing than many might have expected," a review in the *Knoxville News-Sentinel* said on July 26, 2013. "There's a healthy, though not obsessive, emphasis on the harmonies (as in the anthemic

> **Brian is not the only singer to suffer from muscle tension dysphonia (MTD). Shania Twain has been very open about her experience with MTD and how she lost her voice for several years. Ultimately, she took a fifteen-year break from performing.**

RIGHT: Nick and Brian rehearse during soundcheck for their Backstreet Boys' In A World Like This Tour stop in Atlanta, Georgia, on August 22, 2013.

melancholy of 'Permanent Stain'), and dominant lead singer Brian Littrell has improved with age, his thirty-eight-year-old voice resonating with a soulful maturity he simply didn't have in his early twenties."

Just days after *In A World Like This* was released, the tour by the same name began. The tour consisted of 150 shows and lasted for two years, hitting Asia, North America, Europe, South America, Australia, the Middle East, and doing multiple holiday shows. While there are no full, accurate numbers for the entire tour, many shows on the tour were sell-outs, such as the shows in Tuscaloosa, Alabama; Brisbane, Australia; Hamburg, Germany; Montreal, Quebec; and Jacksonville, Florida.

The tour did not come without drama. On the first show, a US show in Chicago, lights and microphones were cut off with five songs to go due to curfew rules. After announcing three shows in Israel in July 2014 that sold out in an hour and a half, Backstreet Boys were forced to postpone

due to the Israel-Gaza conflict. The shows were eventually rescheduled for May 2015.

Critically, the tour gained favorable reviews due to the group performing many of their past hits and showing off their music and vocal chops during an acoustic set.

"Vocally, they also can still belt it out. Their version of early hit 'I'll Never Break Your Heart' was actually quite lovely. And it was easier to appreciate those skills and that harmonizing when they stripped it down mid-set for an acoustic interlude— during which they actually played instruments!—that included a snippet of 'Safest Place to Hide' and the very Bee Gees-esque '10,000 Promises,'" *Calgary Herald* reporter Mike Bell said in the May 17, 2014, edition.

After the *In A World Like This* tour began, Nick had one more thing to celebrate (besides his recent engagement to girlfriend Lauren Kitt)—a new book. *Facing the Music and Living to Talk About It*, released on September 24, 2013, was part memoir and part self-help book, discussing Nick's alcohol and drug addictions and how he got clean. It also featured a foreword by Howie. Nick covered his early life and the tumultuous, unhealthy home environment he grew up in, then talked about becoming a Backstreet Boy, the partying lifestyle, and how partying had almost killed him. He also talked about how he had cleaned himself up, and then turned the question back to the reader, asking how they connected with what Nick had covered in the chapter.

The book hit the *New York Times* Best Seller's list at No. 24 overall (for both print and e-book editions), No. 23 for

When the DVD/Blu-ray of *Show 'Em What You're Made Of* was released on April 28, 2015, it topped Amazon's Music Videos & Constants and Documentary charts, along with peaking at No. 4 on Billboard's Music DVD Chart.

hardcover nonfiction, and No. 19 for e-book nonfiction.

On April 12, 2014, fifteen years to the day that "I Want It That Way" was released as a single, Nick Carter gave up the single life and said, "I do," when he married his longtime girlfriend, Lauren Kitt, at a Santa Barbara, CA, resort. The other four

BELOW: The Boys present Howie with a cake for his fortieth birthday during their In A World Like This Tour stop in Atlanta, Georgia, on August 22, 2013.

Backstreet Boys were in attendance, with Howie being a groomsman and AJ's wife Rochelle as a bridesmaid, and daughter, Ava, the flower girl.

"I'm the youngest [band member] and last to get married," Nick told *Inside Weddings*. "And I could feel how proud they are of me and the love they have for me and Lauren."

BACKSTREET BOYS ON SCREEN

When fans took sail on the 2014 Backstreet Boys cruise, they found out that they would get to see a snippet of the Boys' new documentary, *Show 'Em What You're Made Of*, which had been filmed while recording their latest album and getting ready for the tour. A segment of the documentary was screened that featured the group going to Kevin's hometown and the house he grew up in. When talk turned to Kevin's father's death, tears began flowing throughout the auditorium of the cruise ship.

The documentary, which was shot over the span of two years, was released in full on January 30, 2015, in the United States and a month later in the United Kingdom and Europe. It was later released in the rest of the world.

The documentary also included visits to the other members' hometowns, as well as a stop at the former home of Lou Pearlman. Pearlman's home so haunted Nick that he didn't go inside. Fans also got a look at the Boys living together in London and working in the studio, even hearing songs that never made the album. The documentary also covered rehearsals for the tour. In the midst of it all, fans and viewers learned the true Backstreet Boys story—not the one that appeared in teen magazines.

LEFT: The Boys show the audience the traditional boy band photo pose during the 2014 Backstreet Boys cruise.

OPPOSITE: Kevin and Nick perform during the In A World Like This Tour stop in Atlanta, Georgia, on August 22, 2013.

During Brian's hometown visit, the documentary also covered his vocal issues and one of his visits to therapy to help with them. This led to one of the most intriguing parts of the documentary, when the group and their management were picking songs for the next album. Nick was adamant about including a song called "Soldier," but Brian did not want it on the album. This led to an argument about Brian's voice—specifically if the group and their management team were ever going to really talk about it.

In December 2014, an announcement was made that there would be sneak previews of the documentary at cinemas across the United States on January 29, 2015, just one day before the official release of the documentary on January 30. There was a campaign for fans to get to see the documentary in their local

ABOVE and RIGHT: Kevin and Nick take part in a game show on the 2014 Backstreet Boys cruise.

cinemas. They had to submit an email and their zip code on the website tugg.com. When a list of participating cinemas was listed, fans would get notified. A minimum number of tickets for each screening listed had to be made for the screening to happen. There were 129 screenings for the documentary held on January 29, and the movie made $282,000 from those screenings. The next day, it was available to purchase or watch on-demand through cable and satellite providers, as well as iTunes, Google Play, and Amazon. The digital release topped the Documentary Charts on Google Play and iTunes. To date, it has earned nearly $3 million.

Reviews for the documentary were mostly favorable, currently (2022) holding a 71 percent rating on Rotten Tomatoes with an 83 percent audience score.

"But even if 'Show 'Em What You're Made Of' doesn't answer McLean's essential question of what men do after life as a boy band, the carefully crafted film is an engaging look at how they got to here," Gerrick Kennedy of the *Los Angeles Times* reported on January 29, 2015.

The documentary, in a way, was show-casing the end of an era. But it was also the start of a new era. Soon, the Backstreet Boys would be taking things up a notch and be back on top of the charts.

BELOW: The Backstreet Boys perform "Just To Be Close To You" during the 2014 cruise.

10
WE'VE GOT IT GOIN' ON

"With the twenty-song roster seeing the revival of so many older tunes as well as classic dances and videos, Backstreet Boys: Larger Than Life feels less like a prestige show and more like a celebration—not just of their success from the past two dozen years, but also of the connection they've built with their fans through their music."

—Taylor Weatherby ★ *Billboard*, March 2, 2017

Backstreet Boys perform onstage at the 2016 iHeartRadio Music Festival at T-Mobile Arena on September 24, 2016, in Las Vegas, Nevada.

ABOVE (LEFT TO RIGHT): AJ, Nick, and Brian perform during KTUphoria in Jones Beach, New York, on June 3, 2017.

VIVA LAS VEGAS?

After finishing up the *In A World Like This* tour in 2015 and Nick's time on *Dancing with the Stars*, the Backstreet Boys took a little time off before heading to Europe for their next Backstreet Boys cruise.

Just before the cruise, Nick told *Entertainment Tonight* that the Backstreet Boys had signed a deal for nine shows in Las Vegas as a "test residency." This was one of the big topics of the cruise—that the Boys would be doing something in Las Vegas as their next big project. Besides the rumors, it was known that Kevin and AJ had gone to see Britney Spears perform at Planet Hollywood a few months before.

Less than four months later, it was announced that Backstreet Boys would be taking Las Vegas by storm beginning in March 2017, with an eighteen-date residency at Planet Hollywood Resort & Casino.

"What can you expect from the show?" Brian said in a video promoting the residency. "If you've ever been to a Backstreet Boys show, it's going to be that on steroids."

To many, a Las Vegas residency may have once been the go-to for acts who have been around forever, like the Wayne Newtons or Donnie and Maries of the world, but in the 2010s, Vegas became the place to go. Not only did Britney have an outstanding residency, but so did Celine Dion and Jennifer Lopez. Boyz II Men had also done residencies between tours, and Mariah Carey announced the end of her two-year residency just before the Backstreet Boys announced the start of theirs.

"Introducing the Backstreet Boys into our lineup is another highlight of the company consistently being at the forefront of entertainment and has set a high standard for Las Vegas, one that has forced others in the industry to follow," Jason Gastwirth, senior vice president of marketing and

"God, Your Mama, and Me" was not the Backstreet Boys' first foray into country music. When "Drowning" was released in 2001, two country remixes were also released, which can be found on various Backstreet Boys compilation albums. The music video was also shown on CMT (Country Music Television).

entertainment at Caesars Entertainment, told CNN in a September 23, 2015, article.

Days after announcing their residency, the Backstreet Boys had another surprise for those in Las Vegas—an appearance at the iHeartRadio Festival. The group surprised the crowd by joining country duo Florida Georgia Line on stage to perform "Everybody" before performing other Backstreet Boys hits.

GOING COUNTRY

Tyler Hubbard (Georgia) and Brian Kelley (Florida) of Florida Georgia Line grew up as Backstreet Boys fans and had been performing "Everybody" in concert for years. The Backstreet Boys caught wind of it, and Nick, who was living in Nashville at the time, attended CMA Fest, country music's annual festival, where he met and befriended the guys.

That friendship led to the Backstreet Boys taking their first stab at country music. The group recorded "God, Your Mama, and Me" with Florida Georgia Line, which ended up being on the country duo's *Dig Your Roots*, an album that featured songs with many of the artists they had grown up listening to, like Tim McGraw. Tyler even told fans that his first album was

BELOW: The Backstreet Boys and Florida Georgia Line perform during a taping of *CMT Crossroads* in Franklin, Tennessee, on August 1, 2017.

ABOVE: AJ performs during a radio concert in Atlanta, Georgia, on October 27, 2017.

entered the Hot 100 at No. 92 on March 18, 2017. It was the first time the Backstreet Boys had returned to the chart since 2007's "Inconsolable."

"The ballad's twangy guitars and religious bent is firmly in country territory, yet 'God, Your Mama, and Me' doesn't stray too far from the boy band's pop roots. Is BSB ready for a Nashville rebrand?" Ryan Smith of the *Springfield News-Sun* said in the August 27, 2016, edition of the newspaper.

The accompanying music video was released a month after the single and featured each member with their wives and children.

a Backstreet Boys album, and they were Brian's first show back in Orlando in 1998.

Before *Dig Your Roots* was released on August 26, 2016, more than twenty-five thousand people had bought "God, Your Mama, and Me," making it the fifth most downloaded country song the week of August 29, 2016. The song entered the Hot Country Songs Charts the same week at No. 30 based on the downloads alone, months before it was actually released as a single. The next week it peaked at No. 28.

"To have the Backstreet Boys featured on it was something we kind of envisioned in the studio while recording it," Tyler told *Billboard Magazine* on February 16, 2017. "To have that come to fruition was amazing. It really, really took that song to the next level."

"God, Your Mama, & Me" was officially released to radio on January 23, 2017. It debuted on *Billboard*'s Country Airplay chart at No. 52 five days later and actually

BACKSTREET BOYS: LARGER THAN LIFE

After eight weeks of dance rehearsal and vocal training, the Backstreet Boys opened their ten-week Larger Than Life residency at Planet Hollywood to a sold-out crowd of more than four thousand.

According to Las Vegas' Fox 5 news, Larger Than Life became the fastest-selling Las Vegas residency in history. It was also the first time that Planet Hollywood added two thousand more seats to the venue by opening up the upper deck—something they never did when Britney Spears and Jennifer Lopez were headlining.

The show was a nostalgia-filled two hours, in which the Backstreet Boys performed songs from their early career, including "Undone" from their 2009 album, *This Is Us*. With costume changes, backup dancers, and confetti, it was truly a Las Vegas show.

LEFT: Tracy Parr poses with the Backstreet Boys during their Larger Than Life Las Vegas residency in 2019. ABOVE: The Backstreet Boys celebrate the debut of their Las Vegas residency, Larger Than Life, at the Chateau Nightclub & Rooftop on March 2, 2017, in Las Vegas, Nevada.

BACKSTREET ARMY, ASSEMBLE!

Backstreet Boys mean so much to me because their music saved my life. It's been there when I'm happy, sad, angry, and everywhere in between. There's a Backstreet Boys song for every mood, and it's timeless.

TRACY PARR ★ SUCCASUNNA, NJ
KEEPING THE BACKSTREET PRIDE ALIVE SINCE '96

The show began with each boy in a lighted box that turned around in the air. They wore white, reminiscent of their *Millennium* album cover, and hit the ground running with "Larger Than Life." They continued the upbeat songs by hitting "The One" and "Get Down" before slowing it down a little with "Drowning," "Incomplete," and "Quit Playing Games (With My Heart)." After a wardrobe change, the Boys came back out in black sequin suits to perform "Show Me The Meaning (Of Being Lonely)," "I'll Never Break Your Heart," "Undone," and "As Long As You Love Me."

After another break, they returned in black and red outfits to perform "The Call," "We've Got It Goin' On," and "Get Another Boyfriend" (with AJ's signature "*Good God!*" from the Black & Blue Tour). They slowed it down again for "More Than That" before disappearing into the audience in front of the 200-level seats to perform "All I Have To Give."

After coming back on stage, they performed "Shape of My Heart" before pulling someone on stage to serenade at the end.

For their encore, they would come back out in another outfit to perform "I Want It That Way," and then another encore, "Everybody (Backstreet's Back)."

In the *Vancouver Sun*'s review of *Backstreet's Back* in October 1997, the reviewer says, "Imagine Backstreet Boys twenty years from now. Will you still love them when they're middle-aged men playing Vegas? Didn't think so." The Backstreet Boys' Larger Than Life residency, which began twenty years later in 2017, became one of the best-selling Las Vegas residencies of all time.

"Suckers for synchronized dancing with not be disappointed, and there's pride in seeing Howie D. get into his groove in the second half of the show," Andrea Mandell of *USA Today* said.

For the first nine shows in March 2017, 42,000 of 44,112 (95 percent) seats were sold, bringing in $5.4 million. The second set of shows, a total of eight, sold 34,116 out of 38,267 (89 percent) seats bringing in $4.7 million, making the residency a complete success.

But could more shows be in their future? Absolutely.

In June 2017, the Backstreet Boys announced another run of shows as Planet Hollywood, extending the residency into February 2018.

"We are definitely excited to say we've extended our residency," Howie told *People* on June 9, 2017. "We've been off to a great run! It just feels great to continue this on and hopefully make this into a long-term residency."

The group explained that having three shows a week gave them more time with their families and more time to be creative in and out of the studio, but their favorite part of their show was the fans.

"For the most part, everybody comes to Vegas to have a great time, to party, to

celebrate," Kevin told *People*. "So it's just a great playground for folks to get away and let go, and I think the age of our core fans that grew up with us, where they're at in their lives now, we are a perfect fit for Vegas."

ABOVE: The Boys perform during the Larger Than Life Las Vegas residency on June 15, 2017, in Las Vegas, Nevada.

LEFT: Kevin dances with his wife, Kristin, during the Las Vegas residency on June 17, 2017.

GOD, YOUR MAMA, AND BSB

In April 2017, the Backstreet Boys attended the 52nd Annual Academy of Country Music Awards to perform "God, Your Mama, and Me" with Florida Georgia Line. They were the stars of the red carpet, taking pictures with younger stars such as Lauren Alana to country royalty like Reba McEntire and Rascal Flatts.

The group and duo closed out the awards, with hosts Dierks Bentley and Luke Bryan introducing them. Florida Georgia Line and Backstreet Boys performed their hit song, which was climbing the charts. But when the song ended, something else happened.

"Everybody . . . "

The crowd went wild when the Backstreet Boys began performing "Everybody (Backstreet's Back)." The *Associated Press* said the Backstreet Boys stole the show and called the performance "the night's liveliest moment." Maren Morris, Keith Urban, Nicole Kidman, Faith Hill, Carrie Underwood, and Tim McGraw sang along and danced as Florida Georgia Line joined the group in singing.

But when Brian and Tyler joined the Backstreet Boys in dancing, Tim McGraw was full-on fangirling in the audience.

Two months later, "God, Your Mama, and Me" was the No. 1 country song in the country. It became Florida Georgia Line's thirteenth career No. 1 song, topping both the *Billboard* and Country Aircheck/Media base Country Airplay Charts.

"We're fans of each other, and that's one of the reasons why the song works so well," Nick said in a press release for Florida Georgia Line's label, Big Machine Label Group. "I'm glad it's with these boys that we just reached No. 1 at country radio for the first time."

The Backstreet Boys also joined Florida Georgia Line on tour when the duo added three stadium shows to their 2017 Smooth Tour. They joined Nelly and country singer Chris Lane in Boston at Fenway Park, in Minneapolis at Target Field, and in Chicago at Wrigley Field.

But the arena shows weren't the last time Florida Georgia Line would work

RIGHT: The Boys perform during a radio concert in Atlanta, Georgia, on October 27, 2017.

with the Backstreet Boys. For years, CMT (Country Music Television) had aired *CMT Crossroads*, in which a country artist would perform with an artist from another genre. Previous pairings included Nick Jonas and Thomas Rhett and Taylor Swift and Def Leppard, and now it was going to include Florida Georgia Line and Backstreet Boys.

Just days after the announcement on August 1, 2017, the show was recorded at a small venue in Franklin, TN. It was an invitation-only event.

"Being such fans of each other, this is a really fun way for us to put our mark on our songs," Brian told CMT in a press release on July 25, 2017. "It's going to be a fun night with seven guys who really admire one another. I'm looking forward to what comes of it!"

Fans of both groups were lucky enough to watch the two powerhouses perform each other's songs. Florida Georgia Line took some of the leads from "All I Have to Give" and "As Long As You Love Me," while Backstreet Boys showcased their vocals on Florida Georgia Line's hits "H.O.L.Y." and "Cruise."

All seven of the performers' vocals got to shine on songs before performing "Everybody (Backstreet's Back)," where Florida Georgia Line joined the group in their iconic dance.

"Getting us all under one roof in Nashville will be fire," Tyler told CMT. "We can't wait to jump in on each other's songs and add our flavor to ones we grew up listening to."

After the special aired on August 31, 2017, both groups saw an increase in sales on iTunes for songs that were performed on the show. According to *Music Row*

According to *Music Row Magazine*, the Backstreet Boys and Florida Georgia Line's *CMT Crossroads* special earned the show its highest ratings in more than five years, since Steven Tyler and Carrie Underwood performed together in 2012.

Magazine, the Backstreet Boys reported a 22 percent increase in streaming overall.

Backstreet Boys would go on to perform for Florida Georgia Line a few months later when the duo was named one of CMT's Artists of the Year for 2017. They performed the duo's hit song "H.O.L.Y." with all five Backstreet Boys taking lead on a different part of the song and Kevin playing the piano.

"Simply put, we're family now," Kevin told CMT about the performance. "And it's an honor to recognize our brothers with their fifth CMT Artist of the Year trophy."

BELOW: The Boys perform an acoustic concert during the 2016 Backstreet Boys European cruise.

11
BACKSTREET'S BACK

....

"I remember waiting for the Backstreet Boys to arrive on set for their 2017 *PAPER* cover shoot and interview during their Las Vegas residency. Suddenly, the doors swung open and AJ entered. It was one of those moments where the air in the room seemed to change. As the rest of the Boys came in, it was clear that after all of those years, their star power and their 'It factor' burned as bright as ever."

—Abby Schreiber ★ former Executive Editor of *PAPER* Magazine ★ interviewed the group for their 2017 cover story

The Backstreet Boys perform "I'll Never Break Your Heart" during their Larger Than Life Las Vegas residency in Las Vegas, Nevada, on October 26, 2018.

TWENTY-FIVE YEARS

ABOVE and RIGHT: The Boys perform the entire *Millennium* album on Millennium Night on the 2018 Backstreet Boys cruise. Fans all dressed in white to celebrate the album.

Just after celebrating their twenty-fifth anniversary together, the Backstreet Boys took to the seas once again for another Backstreet Boys cruise celebrating the milestone. This time, things were a little different—the Boys had some new material to share.

Fans were separated into two different groups because of the size of the auditorium, and phones and cameras were confiscated before they attended a listening session with Kevin to hear some of the new material that the Boys were working on. Among the songs played were "Passionate," which fans began rallying behind to make the album; "Just Like You Like It," which had a country twang; a sweet mid-tempo song called "Is It Just Me"; and

one that Kevin kept accidentally playing that the fans named "Three Words." Kevin also played a song called "Lion in My Bed," which piqued fans' interest, and "The Way It Was," a track showcasing Nick's vocals and a retro chorus.

Fans learned that they would be getting a new Backstreet Boys song soon, except they didn't realize how soon.

Two weeks after the cruise, the Boys began a teaser countdown on social media that lasted for three days. Finally, they announced that the first single from their upcoming ninth studio album would be released on May 17, 2018. The song, called "Don't Go Breaking My Heart," was their first new song in five years.

It was also announced that they had signed with RCA Records, their first record deal since leaving Jive Records in 2011.

"The minute we heard this song, we knew it was special," Kevin said in a press release from RCA Records. "I geeked out over the piano and synths. When that groove drops on the second verse, COME ON. Great verse, hook, and melodies. Just makes you want to listen over and over again."

"We've had a lot of love from the country world lately, so we definitely explored that and at one point even talked about doing a straight-up country record," Howie said in

On the 2018 Backstreet Boys cruise, the Boys dressed up as the Spice Girls on '90s theme night. Nick (Baby), Howie (Ginger), AJ (Scary), Kevin (Posh), and Brian (Sporty) dressed in the complete getup, down to the heels and stuffed bras, taking the stage to cheers and laughter from fans.

a May 17, 2018, article in *Metro*. "Not to say that isn't still on the table and something we'll consider down the line, but we kept coming back to the fact that our roots remain in the pop world."

"Don't Go Breaking My Heart" was written by Stuart Crichton, Jamie Hartman, and Stephen Wrabel and produced by both Hartman and Crichton. It was a new sound for the group, and critics loved it.

"We honestly never thought we'd be writing this in 2018, but we're looking

BELOW: The Boys sing on stage dressed as the Spice Girls during the 2018 Backstreet Boys cruise.

forward to hearing what else the Backstreet Boys have to offer on the upcoming album," Parker Hall of *Digital Trends* said on May 17, 2018.

While the song was considered a "comeback single" and the group was "reuniting" (they weren't), the song was the first time that the Backstreet Boys charted on *Billboard*'s Adult Contemporary, Hot 100, and Mainstream Top 40 charts since "Inconsolable" in 2006—twelve years prior. It also appeared on the Radio Songs chart, peaking at No. 38, the first time since the band released "Incomplete" in 2005.

Overall, the song was a success. It reached No. 1 in China and was a Top 5 hit in Sri Lanka. It was also a hit in the US, reaching No. 8 on the Adult Contemporary chart, No. 9 on the Adult Top 40 chart, No. 17 on the Dance Club Songs, No. 18 on the Mainstream Top 40 chart, No. 28 on the Dance/Mix Show Airplay chart, and No. 63 on the *Billboard* Hot 100. *Billboard*'s

year-end charts ranked No. 19 on the Adult Contemporary chart and No. 28 on the Adult Top 40 chart. The song went gold in both Australia and Canada.

A major feat was their No. 8 position on the US Adult Contemporary chart. It surpassed "I Want It That Way," which only made it to No. 11 in 1999.

The music video for the song was directed by Rich+Tone, who frequently choreographed their shows and also worked as background dancers on the Into the Millennium Tour.

BELOW and RIGHT: Nick and Kevin celebrate the kickoff of the 2018 Backstreet Boys cruise in Miami, Florida, on May 3, 2018.

Jennie poses with the Backstreet Boys during the In A World Like This Tour in Wantagh, New York, in August 2013. It was her first picture with all five Backstreet Boys.

BACKSTREET ARMY, ASSEMBLE!

There really is no way to adequately describe how I feel about the Backstreet Boys. To put it plainly, I would not be me without AJ, Brian, Kevin, Nick, and Howie. Individually and as a group, the Boys have left their mark on my life.

I "officially" became a fan in 1999. I was eleven, and now I am thirty-four; Nick was nineteen, now he is forty-two. I did not just grow up being a fan of the Boys. I grew up with the Boys. While the world around me has changed, the Boys have been a constant in my life for the last twenty-something years.

The Backstreet Boys have been and continue to be a great source of joy and comfort for me. I can always rely on their music to cheer me up, put a smile on my face, or calm me down. No matter what is going on in my life, I can always put on their music and be right where I need to be. It has been that way since I bought *Millennium*.

Over the years, I have been lucky. I have had the opportunity to see (and meet) the Boys on numerous occasions. And yet each time, I still get excited, I still get nervous, and I still cannot wait to see what comes next.

JENNIE S. ★ MASSAPEQUA, NY
KEEPING THE BACKSTREET PRIDE ALIVE SINCE '99

ABOVE: The Boys and Florida Georgia Line accept an award onstage at the 2018 CMT Music Awards at Bridgestone Arena in Nashville, Tennessee, on June 6, 2018.

AND THE AWARD GOES TO . . .

Shortly after the release of "Don't Go Breaking My Heart," the Backstreet Boys were nominated for a CMT Award for their performance of "Everybody (Backstreet's Back)" with Florida Georgia Line on *CMT Crossroads*. They were also invited to Nashville for the award ceremony, where they presented an award and got to perform "Don't Go Breaking My Heart" for the first time live on television.

By the end of the night, the Boys were winners.

"So who would have thought that twenty years ago when 'Everybody (Backstreet's Back)' came out, that these guys, Florida Georgia Line, would be singing it on stage and we would actually do something together," Brian said while accepting the award.

"I gotta say, I wanna thank God, your mama, and these boys right here," Nick said jokingly, pointing to Florida Georgia Line as the crowd cheered.

While some country music loyalists didn't like the fact that the Backstreet Boys won the award, even if it was with Florida Georgia Line, and performed, the Boys' performance of "Don't Go Breaking My Heart" went over well with the crowd and critics.

"In a stripped-down performance with their trademark choreography (and lots of fog machine action), they showed they haven't missed a step since we last saw them live," Brian Haas of *Entertainment Tonight* said on June 6, 2018.

MORE VEGAS

In July 2018, the Backstreet Boys released more Las Vegas dates—and their final dates, at that. With shows already happening that July and August, more dates in October and November were planned, along with the final run in February and April 2019.

For the new dates, the band did change the show just a smidge by adding "Don't Go Breaking My Heart" to the setlist before the encore of "Everybody (Backstreet's Back)."

According to Caesars Entertainment and Live Nation, at that point, the residency had made more than $23 million and was seen by over 185,000 guests.

"What started with eighteen shows has grown into an unforgettable experience for us," Howie said in a press release on July 11, 2018. "We will always be thankful to this show, the fans who have flown in from all over the world to see this show, and to Las Vegas."

With "Don't Go Breaking My Heart" being a success, after finishing the August Vegas dates, the Backstreet Boys were invited to perform at the MTV Video Music Awards preshow and present an award on the show.

BELOW: The Boys talk to the audience during their record-breaking Larger Than Life Las Vegas residency in Las Vegas, Nevada, on October 26, 2018.

WHAT ARE THE CHANCES?

On November 9, 2018, the Backstreet Boys released "Chances," their second single from their upcoming album. The song, written by Ryan Tedder, Shawn Mendes, Fiona Bevan, Casey Smith, Geoff Warburton, and Scott Harris, was produced by Ryan and Zach Skelton. The verses of the song are mid-tempo, but the chorus takes it up a notch with pumping, danceable synthesizers.

Taylor Weatherby of *Billboard* called "Chances" a "thumping love song that allows all five Backstreet Boys' voices to shine on their own."

"Lyrically, the song, it's not your typical Backstreet Boys love song, which is something we all really liked," AJ told *Billboard* in the same article. "It's more of that realistic love story about chance, to find that person in the most precarious of scenarios. It's a really beautiful love song."

The song peaked at No. 7 on the US *Billboard* Bubbling Under Hot 100 chart two weeks later, on November 24, 2018. It reached No. 19 on *Billboard*'s Adult Top 40 chart and No. 9 on the US Dance Club Songs with the remixes that were released that January. It peaked at only No. 55 on the Canadian Hot 100 chart but was certified gold in Canada.

The music video was directed by AJ and his longtime friend René Elizondo Jr. and was filmed at Union Station in Los Angeles.

BELOW: The Boys perform at the 2018 CMT Music Awards.

LEFT: Another award show appearance! The Boys perform onstage during the 2018 MTV Video Music Awards Pre-Show at Radio City Music Hall on August 20, 2018, in New York.

Filming for the video meant long hours, shooting from 2:00 p.m. until 4:00 a.m. It featured a dance sequence by two students from the Glorya Kaufman School of Dance at the University of South California. The female dancer, Madison Vomastek, just happened to be a Backstreet Boys fan.

"I remember listening to Backstreet Boys with my older cousin Grace, in her room with her fabulous cheetah-print couch, and thinking that they were the definition of cool," Madison said in a student blog post at her school on November 15, 2018. "Meeting and performing with them reassured my childhood notions, and they exceeded my expectations. Each one of them, Brian, Howie, AJ, Kevin, and Nick, is an artist on his own and has such a giving heart. I was lucky to not feel like just a body in the video, but a vital piece of the puzzle."

IT'S IN OUR DNA

The beginning of November 2018 was an exciting time for fans. Not only did they get a new single, "Chances," but a new album and tour announcement—their biggest tour in eighteen years.

It was announced that *DNA*, their tenth studio album, would be released on January 25, 2019. It would be their first album on RCA Records and would feature their latest two singles, plus songs written by singer Andy Grammer and country singer Dustin Lynch.

"We always talk about quality versus quantity any time we do something," Brian told Albany, NY's *Times Union* newspaper in July 2022. *DNA* is our tenth album, and it's great from top-to-bottom, a quality album that we know stands the test of time. We're so proud of it, we said, 'let's tour and give the fans what they want.'"

Along with the album announcement, the Backstreet Boys announced the DNA World Tour, their first since the In A World Like This Tour ended in 2015. The tour would start in the UK and Europe, with the first date in Lisbon, Portugal, in May and run through the end of June. The North American leg would start on July 12, 2019, in Washington, DC, ending in September in Newark, NJ.

"The journey is ongoing with us, and there is so much left to do," Brian said in a press release from RCA Records. "We're living the next chapter that hasn't been told yet, and that's exciting."

One exciting aspect, which was new for Backstreet Boys fans, was that those who purchased concert tickets received a free physical copy of *DNA* once it was released.

"We were able to bring all of our influences and styles into one coherent piece of work," Kevin said in the press release. "These songs are a great representation of who we are as individuals and who we are as a group. It's our DNA."

On January 4, 2019, the Backstreet Boys celebrated the new year with a new song, "No Place." The third single from the upcoming *DNA* was written by award-winning country songwriters Brett James, Joshua Miller, and Troy Verges.

"You know, when myself and Kevin and Howie were sharing an apartment together, yeah, I wouldn't sing about 'No Place,'" Brian told *Bustle* in a February 27, 2019, article about how much their music has changed. "We're all fathers, and we have a reason to go to work every day. We have a reason to love and be passionate about what we do."

"No Place" debuted on the *Billboard* Adult Contemporary Chart and spent five weeks on the chart, peaking at No. 27.

The music video wasn't the first time that all the Boys' wives were in a video (they were featured in their duet with Florida Georgia Line), but it was the first time that all of their children (that had been born by that time) were featured.

A NO.1 ALBUM, A SUPER BOWL COMMERCIAL, AND A GRAMMY NOMINATION

When the Backstreet Boys returned to their Vegas residency in the first week of February 2019, it was also the week that *DNA* debuted at No. 1 on the *Billboard* 200 charts. It was their first No. 1 album since *Black & Blue* spent two weeks at No. 1 in December 2000. The album sold 234,000 equivalent album units (with 6.6 million streams) in the US for the last week of January 2019. Of those units, 227,000 of

them were physical album sales, which are weighted more heavily than streams.

According to *Billboard*, it was the longest gap between No. 1 albums since the year before, when Paul McCartney returned to the top of the charts after thirty-six years. The group also had the largest sales week since Carrie Underwood's *Cry Pretty* sold 251,000 copies in its first week in September 2018. Accounting for a lot of the sales were the albums that fans had been promised when purchasing tour tickets through Live Nation or Ticketmaster the previous November.

In Canada, the album debuted at No. 1 with over 46,000 first-week sales and was certified platinum almost a year later. *DNA*

also debuted at No. 1 in Austria, Japan, and Switzerland and was a Top 5 hit in Australia, Belgium, the Netherlands, Germany, Portugal, Scotland, Spain, and the United Kingdom (as a digital album).

Critically, *DNA* was a success.

"Across *DNA*'s 12 tracks, Backstreet Boys succeed in keeping your attention and reminding you why they're still here over two decades later," Pip Ellwood-Hughes of *Entertainment Focus* said on January 25, 2019. "At the heart of the music has always been those killer harmonies, and they make sure to hang every song on them."

"The variety of sound is also a testament to the Backstreet Boys' progression,

ABOVE: The Boys walk the red carpet at the 61st Annual Grammy Awards at Staples Center on February 10, 2019 in Los Angeles, California.

showing that they're not afraid to push boundaries to find their lane in today's pop sphere," Taylor Weatherby of *Billboard* said on January 25, 2019.

"The way they launched *DNA* was really smart and strategic," Backstreet Boys fan and marketing expert Danielle Spurge of Virginia Beach, VA, said. "They know their fans well enough to know what appeals to them, but they also know they need to reach new people, and I think the way they launched *DNA* successfully did both of those things. They are smart to leverage their past success and still aim to create new experiences and milestones for themselves and fans."

When it came to Super Bowl LIII, there were more important things to talk about than the New England Patriots beating the Los Angeles Rams. The 2019 Super Bowl gave the world one of the finest Super Bowl commercials ever to be made—the Backstreet Boys and Chance the Rapper promoting Doritos' "Now It's Hot" campaign.

THE GRAMMY MUSEUM® PRESENTS
BACKSTREET BOYS THE EXPERIENCE

EXHIBIT OPEN
APRIL 10 - SEPTEMBER 2

PRESENTED BY: blue

RECORDING ACADEMY
GRAMMY MUSEUM
TICKETS AVAILABLE AT
GRAMMYMUSEUM.ORG

Teases first came out on January 17, 2019, with Chance the Rapper posing with denim-clad Backstreet Boys, trying to find a place to pose. The Backstreet Boys then flew to Atlanta the Friday before the Sunday game to do press, not only for the new album and upcoming tour but for their partnership with Chance and Doritos.

"We're honored to be here. We did a commercial with Chance the Rapper for Doritos Flamin' Hot Nachos. He took the original, the classic, and put some fire on it, and Flamin' Hot Nachos did a remix of 'I Want It That Way,' and you're going to see it on the Super Bowl," Kevin

told Atlanta's 11 Alive news at the press conference on February 1, 2019.

The commercial was named one of the best during the lackluster Super Bowl, and Backstreet Boys were still riding high with the new album release.

"And hopefully, this Sunday, we take home our first Grammy," AJ said in Las Vegas during their first residency show of the year on February 6, 2019. The group had been nominated for Best Pop Duo/ Group Performance for "Don't Go Breaking My Heart," their first nomination since 2002. "We are truly, truly blessed, and again, hats off to each and every one of you, because without you guys, the most amazing fans in the entire world, we would not do what we do and would not still be here twenty-six years later."

The weekend after *DNA* debuted at No. 1, the Backstreet Boys went to Los Angeles after their Saturday evening show in Las Vegas to attend the 2019 Grammy Awards.

"It's been a while. It's exciting. It's an honor. No matter what happens tonight, it's a celebration," Kevin told *Entertainment Tonight* on February 10, 2019. "We've always wanted a career. We love music. We're music fans. We put a lot of work, passion, and heart into what we do. I think that by us being nominated twenty-six years into the game, it's showing and paying dividends, and we're just honored. It's a celebration and privilege. Just keep grinding. Keep working hard and believe."

The Backstreet Boys were up against Christina Aguilera featuring Demi Lovato ("Fall in Line"), Tony Bennett and Diana Krall ("'S Wonderful"), Lady Gaga and Bradley Cooper ("Shallow"), Maroon 5 featuring Cardi B ("Girls Like You"), Justin Timberlake featuring Chris Stapleton ("Say Something"), and Zedd, Maren Morris, and Grey ("The Middle"). Ultimately, the award went to "Shallow" by Lady Gaga and Bradley Cooper, from their movie, *A Star Is Born*.

While the Backstreet Boys didn't win their Grammy Award in 2019, they did get a whole experience at the Grammy Museum in Los Angeles. Between April 10 and September 2, 2019, the Grammy Museum held "Backstreet Boys: The Experience," where fans could get a one-of-a-kind fan experience, celebrating over twenty-six years together with personal memorabilia and artwork, photography, and wardrobe. The exhibit also included interactive experiences where you could take a photo with the group as well as a wall of nothing but photos of fans with the Backstreet Boys.

"The Backstreet Boys re-defined pop music as we know it creating a dedicated fan phenomenon that still exists almost thirty years later," Michael Sticka, the Grammy Museum's executive director, said in a press release. "We're thrilled to celebrate the group's unique commitment to their fans and vice versa while producing a one-of-a-kind immersive interactive experience."

BYE BYE, VEGAS

With the DNA World Tour starting up in May, the Backstreet Boys ended their Las Vegas residency on April 27, 2019, with one last show at Zappos Theater at Planet Hollywood.

The show, which was sold out on a regular basis, was sold out again on the final night. It was an emotional evening for Nick, AJ, Brian, Kevin, and Howie.

"It's been pretty incredible," AJ told the crowd at the show. "On behalf of myself and the Boys, I want to thank everybody here that's made this two-year journey so pleasurable."

During "Shape of My Heart," a fan or another celebrity in the crowd would usually be brought on stage to be serenaded, but on the final night, the guys brought their wives onto the stage and handed them a rose while on bended knees.

"I'm not going to get emotional. I'm not going to cry," Brian told the crowd. "I'd like to, because you guys have honestly blessed our lives so much."

BELOW: Nick performs during the Larger Than Life Las Vegas residency in Las Vegas, Nevada, on October 26, 2018.

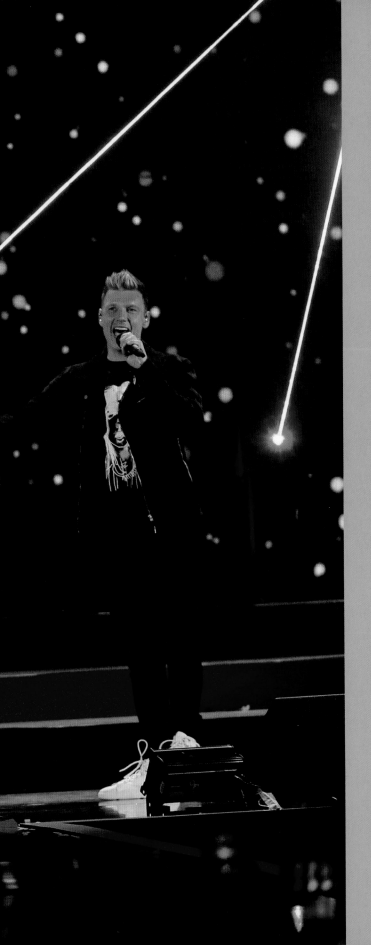

12
WEIRD WORLD

"Most fans have since grown up and adapted to lives that didn't culminate in marrying Nick Carter, but the Boys still evoke the same deep emotion. After 70-odd Backstreet Boys shows, I shed my first concert tear hearing the opening chords of 'Don't Wanna Lose You Now,' having previously given up hope of ever seeing such an old favorite live."

—Leena Tailor, ★ *Variety* ★ August 7, 2019

The Boys perform during the iHeartRadio Music Festival at T-Mobile Arena in Las Vegas, Nevada, on September 20, 2019.

ABOVE: Nick raises the houselights to see the audience during the DNA World Tour stop in Birmingham, Alabama, on September 4, 2019.

DNA WORLD TOUR KICKS OFF

"The Backstreet Boys returned to Madrid last night with their DNA World Tour. The legendary '90s band filled the WiZink Center, causing the stands and the track to bramble with the assistance of nearly fifteen thousand fans. Women and men between the ages of their late twenties and forties relived their youthful days," ABC Culture in Madrid, Spain, reported on May 14, 2019, just after the Backstreet Boys' second stop on their DNA World Tour.

And that's how most of the DNA World Tour went in Europe, where the group had not toured officially since the In A World Like This Tour.

"Backstreet Boys delivered all their hits, perfect sound, dynamic staging, and some lovely moments with the adoring crowds clustered around the stage. It was pop perfection," Stefan Kyriazis of *Express* said in a June 19, 2019, review of one of the London shows at the O2.

"Two sold-out nights at the O2 again for the Backstreet Boys. Does this mean you still love us?" Nick asked the crowd, according to the review. It was obvious that they did.

According to *Broadway World*, the Backstreet Boys sold over 350,000 tickets across Europe, and fans were already hungry for more shows.

When the tour hit the United States in Washington, DC, on July 12, 2019, the reaction was the same. And it was repeated again a few days later, when they played to a packed house of 16,784 fans at the Bell Centre in Montreal on July 15, 2019.

"It was the kind of evening that could be called a love-in, as band and fans

LEFT: AJ and Brian perform during their DNA World Tour stop in Birmingham, Alabama, on September 4, 2019.

The Backstreet Boys perform "The One" during their DNA World Tour stop in Birmingham, Alabama, on September 4, 2019.

commuted on song after song during the generous, two-hour set. They would eventually get to amped-up showstopper 'Everybody (Backstreet's Back).' Truth is, they never really left," T'Cha Dunlevy of the *Montreal Gazette* reported.

One thing was for certain—the fans were not the same fans they were back in 1999. Throughout the tour, bras and panties were flung on stage during the more fun, interactive parts of the show. In Houston, one fan tossed a bra at Brian, who exclaimed that they "still got it!"

The Backstreet Boys still had it with journalists too. Reviews for the tour were raves.

"The Boys promoted this tour as the biggest Backstreet outing in eighteen years, since flying through the audience on harnesses during the 'Millennium' era. And while not overbearing in pyrotechnics or flying pop singers, it did play healthy tribute to the group's mark on pop music without being too heavy-banded in nostalgia," Matthew Leimkuehler of the *Tennessean* said on August 27, 2019.

According to Pollstar's 2019 Year End Worldwide Ticket Sales, the Backstreet Boys came in at No. 10, selling 1,070,669 tickets and making $100,178,801 in ticket sales. In the United States alone, they sold 651,515 tickets.

BELOW LEFT: Nick and Brian make the "shape of their heart" during the DNA World Tour stop in Pittsburgh, Pennsylvania, on September 14, 2019.

BELOW RIGHT: AJ performs during the DNA World Tour stop in Washington, DC, on July 12, 2019.

Christel poses with the Backstreet Boys at the DNA World Tour on September 5, 2022, at Jiffy Lube Live in Bristow, VA.

BACKSTREET ARMY, ASSEMBLE!

I have been a Backstreet Boys fan for close to twenty-five years. They are one of my longest relationships. Like most relationships, there are highs and lows, but I'll always come back. What brings me back? The friends I've made are like family—witnessing the beautiful brotherhood between these men. Of course, the music, talent, and performances that I will always cherish. More than the things I listed that are tangible, there is the feeling of coming home. The Backstreet Boys have fostered a fandom not just with their talent and good looks but with their openness and vulnerability. They have shared the highs and lows with us and, by doing that, made us "fans," in a way, a part of their family. The Boys famously sang, "As long as there'll be music, we'll be coming back again," and I know I will be right there every time.

CHRISTEL M. ★ WASHINGTON, DC
KEEPING THE BACKSTREET PRIDE ALIVE SINCE '97

ABOVE: The Boys during their DNA World Tour stop in Washington, DC, on July 12, 2019.

RIGHT: Nick and Brian perform during the DNA World Tour stop in Pittsburgh, Pennsylvania, on September 14, 2019.

The DNA World Tour ended up being the Backstreet Boys' most successful tour since Black & Blue in 2000, and they had only just finished the first leg.

LET IT BE ME

Another day, another collaboration. After the massive success of their country hit "God, Your Mama, and Me" with Florida Georgia Line, the Backstreet Boys released a song with DJ and producer Steve Aoki.

"Let It Be Me," a mid-tempo ballad with EDM beats and lyrics about love and acceptance, and written by Steve Aoki, Teddy Geiger, Dan Hening, Gazzo, Jake Torrey, Noah Conrad, and Alexandru

Cracium, was released on September 6, 2019.

The song came to fruition after Nick joined Steve in Las Vegas at Hakkassan to perform "Everybody (Backstreet's Back)." Steve, who also lived in Las Vegas, then invited Nick and the other Backstreet Boys over to his home studio.

"Being able to work with these guys was so organic and effortless," Steve said in a press release. "Collaborating with a group that I've been listening to since I was a kid was such a memorable moment for me. This song has a beautiful message and relates to a lot of different people overcoming challenges when you love someone, and love always wins in the end. I'm really proud of this one and know it will touch a lot of people."

Reviews for "Let It Be Me" were terrific, especially for the music video. The video, directed by Tyler Dunning Evans, featured visuals of the Backstreet Boys and Steve Aoki singing, but also with a handful of people sharing their personal stories of overcoming challenges, heartbreak, and

ABOVE: The Backstreet Boys bow at the end of their DNA World Tour stop in Newark, New Jersey, on September 15, 2019.

love, from discovering their sexuality to dealing with the loss of a loved one.

"The message behind it is one we think everyone can relate to. It's about working through any challenge that life brings to be with the person you love," the Backstreet Boys said in a press release. "And the importance of that message is something we really tried to show with the music video by having real couples tell their story."

In every interview he did, Steve could not stop talking about how amazing it was to work with Nick, Kevin, AJ, Brian, and Howie.

"These guys are just . . . like in the studio working with them, they're down to earth, they're hungry, they want to make sure it's

the best version, and they're professional. They're awesome to work with, absolutely incredible to work with," Steve told iHeartRadio.

After the last show on the US leg of the DNA World Tour, a makeup date in Hershey, PA, after the original was postponed due to thunderstorms, the Backstreet Boys headed back to good ol' Las Vegas for a surprise performance with Steve during the iHeart Music Festival.

At first, the music video began to play on the screen behind Steve, who was at his turntable, with the people in the video talking about what they were going through. Then the Backstreet Boys walked out to sing, with the people's stories still playing out

LEFT: AJ and Nick join Joey Fatone and Lance Bass of *NSYNC at Bingo Under The Stars, in celebration of Pride, at The Grove in Los Angeles on June 18, 2021.

OPPOSITE: Nick performs during the DNA World Tour stop in Washington, DC, on July 12, 2019.

Fans got a Christmas surprise on December 18, 2020, when the Backstreet Boys appeared on a song with the Queen of Pop, Britney Spears. The sultry song, "Matches," appeared on a rerelease of her album, *Glory*, and marked the first time that the former Jive Records artists released a song together. The song had originally been recorded for *DNA*, but hadn't made the final track listing, so Britney decided to record it herself and keep the Boys' vocals.

behind them on the screen. At the end of the song, the same people from the video walked out on stage with the performers to show the obstacles they had overcome for love.

On the Canadian Adult Contemporary charts, "Let It Be Me" spent five weeks on the chart, peaking at No. 36. In the US, on *Billboard*'s Dance/Mix Show Airplay chart, the song spent fifteen weeks on the chart, peaking at No. 4.

CLOSING OUT 2019

To say that 2019 was a stellar year for the Backstreet Boys is an understatement. With a No. 1 album, a Grammy nomination, and a nearly sold-out arena tour in Europe and North America, they ended it just like they started it—on stage.

After promotion for their Steve Aoki single, the Backstreet Boys headed to Asia just two weeks after the birth of Nick's daughter, Saoirse.

Starting out in Osaka, Japan, and traveling all the way to Singapore, the Backstreet Boys performed in front of over sixty-three thousand fans in just six shows. For their last show in Singapore, they performed before a sold-out crowd of ten thousand at the Singapore Indoor Stadium.

"Many will say that this is a concert befitting the most successful boy band of all time. Between sincere speeches from every single member about their own families and babies and reminiscing about how they started a massive twenty-six years ago, who wouldn't agree?" Genevieve Sarah Loh of Channel News Asia reported on October 31, 2019. "Especially when the Boys break out in a cappella and prove that, despite tired touring voices, they can still hit the very notes and harmonies that made the world swoon."

Once the Asia tour was over, the Backstreet Boys went to Hawaii for four shows to really put a close to the 2019 edition of the DNA World Tour. Though they had performed in Hawaii for the 2006 NFL Pro Bowl halftime show, this was the first time that the Backstreet Boys would be putting on a concert in the Aloha State.

The shows, played at the historic Blaisdell Arena where Elvis Presley's "Aloha from Hawaii via Satellite" was held back in 1973, were played in front of more than twenty-three thousand fans—almost completely sold-out crowds. Fans from Hawaii got the first crack at tickets for the show, but fans from around the world also flew to the vacation destination to take in the sights and the Backstreet Boys.

HELLO, 2020, AND HELLO, SOUTH AMERICA!

As 2020 began, the Backstreet Boys were taking some well-deserved time off. But before too long, they would be heading to Mexico and then South America to kick off the 2020 edition of the DNA World Tour.

Before leaving, they announced dates for Australia and New Zealand, plus more North American shows. Instead of arenas, they would be performing out outdoor venues.

The next leg of the tour started with six shows in Mexico, including three shows in Mexico City at the Palacio de los Deportes, where the group played in front of sold-out crowds of more than forty-three thousand. Newspaper articles about the three shows in Mexico City said "fans who attended were euphoric," and the building shook with screams.

After two shows in Monterrey, where they played in front of 25,500 fans, they stopped in Guadalajara before making their way to Costa Rica for the very first time. When tickets had first gone on sale for the Costa Rica show the previous September, tickets closest to the stage had sold out in ten minutes, with other areas selling out in a few hours.

The Backstreet Boys made their way to South America, performing two shows in Colombia and two shows in Chile. The tour then made its way to Buenos Aires, Argentina, where the show was seen by more than just the thirty thousand people

at the concert—it was also broadcast live online for fans around the world to see.

But as the tour continued, something else was happening in the world. On March 11, the World Health Organization declared that COVID-19 (an abbreviated version of the official name, coronavirus disease 2019) was a pandemic. That same day, the NBA suspended their entire 2020 season. Two days later, President Donald J. Trump declared a national emergency in the United States.

That night, the Backstreet Boys performed in Rio de Janeiro, Brazil, at Jeunesse Arena, in what would be their last concert for over two years. A day later, the Backstreet Boys canceled their show in Sao Paolo, Brazil, and were on their way home to the United States.

"We regret to announce that in accordance with recent restrictions recommended by the Governor of the State of Sao Paulo, the Backstreet Boys show scheduled to take place on Sunday, March 15, at Allianz Parque has been postponed. The safety and well-being of our fans, employees, and all personnel is always our top priority. We regret the disappointment to fans," the Backstreet Boys said in a social media post on March 14, 2020.

LOCKDOWN

The day after the Backstreet Boys left Brazil, certain US states began to shut down to prevent the spread of COVID-19. The Centers for Disease Control issued a "No Sail Order" to cruise ships. Businesses began to let employees work from home if they were able to. Schools shut down, including New York City's public school system, the biggest in the country. Toilet paper became scarce at grocery stores around the world. The United States and Canada suspended nonessential travel between the two countries. California issued a "stay-at-home" order for all forty million of the state's residents.

And like the rest of us, the Backstreet Boys were at their respective homes doing what the rest of the world was doing—hunkering down. But, as they tend to do, they tried to keep people's spirits up, even at the beginning of the pandemic.

One of the things they did was work with Jennifer Garner and Amy Adams's #SaveWithStories initiative, which helped raise money for food banks and mobile meal trucks through partnerships with Save the Children and No Kid Hungry. AJ, Nick, and Howie read *Click, Clack, Moo: Cows That Type* by Doreen Cronin in a video posted on social media.

Near the end of March, the Backstreet Boys did something that hadn't been done on television before—perform from five different locations across the country for Elton John's iHeartRadio's Living Room Concert for America on FOX. No pandemic or social distancing was going to stop the Backstreet Boys from performing their hit song, "I Want It That Way." Nick performed from his home in Las Vegas, NV, while Brian tuned in from Atlanta, GA, Howie from Orlando, FL, and AJ and Kevin from Los Angeles, CA.

The media ate the performance up.

"The Backstreet Boys' 21-year-old(!) song, which topped the *Billboard* charts at No. 11 on October 12, 1999, tugged on the nostalgic feel-good heartstrings exactly the way cooped-up Americans

BELOW: The Boys perform—in five different locations—during *Fox Presents the iHeart Living Room Concert for America* on March 29, 2020, to provide entertainment relief and support for Americans during the COVID-19 pandemic.

OPPOSITE: Nick rehearses for the upcoming show the After Party at the Venetian Resort on August 19, 2021, in Las Vegas.

ABOVE: AJ masks up in Los Angeles in November 2020.

about trying and failing to be close to someone, somehow brought me to a weird breaking point that I didn't know I had. *NSYNC could never," Claire Landsbaum of *Vanity Fair* said after watching the performance.

The group continued to try to shine light and positivity via social media, whether it was sending video messages to health care workers, posting clips of Kevin trying to do the "As Long As You Love Me" chair dance in a sumo wrestler outfit from the 2018 Backstreet Boys cruise, or holding virtual visits with patients at children's hospitals.

However, after two months of lockdown, fans' worst fears came true— the 2020 DNA World Tour was going to be postponed indefinitely.

"As much as we were hoping to see you guys this summer, due to the state of this entire world, facing this pandemic, unfortunately, we have to postpone the summer tour," AJ said in a video message to fans.

"I know, it hits us all where we don't want it to hit," Brian continued in the video. "But at the end of the day, safety is the number one priority. Our fans are the number one priority, and the best thing we can do is take care of ourselves and our loved ones right now." Eight days later, the band announced rescheduled dates for 2021.

Barbara Di Mattia, a fan from Italy, had just seen Nick at the 2019 German Comic Con in December. She didn't think COVID-19 would be a big deal and life would get back to normal.

"If I was calm and composed at first, I quickly became hopeless and depressed. Traveling to see the Boys and my friends

were unknowingly craving, filling up Instagram Stories and Twitter feeds of both boy band aficionados and former skeptics alike," Rachel Chang of *Forbes* said on March 30, 2020.

"But seeing them together, singing a song from simpler times that is literally

have always been my source of happiness, but being so far away this time wasn't easy," Barbara said.

STAYING IN TOUCH

With the rest of the 2020 DNA World Tour not happening, the Backstreet Boys found other things to do and try to stay connected with fans.

"Being a fan during COVID was bittersweet," Medina Goudelock of Pennsylvania said. "I had become used to seeing them quite often during their Vegas residency, and now I had no idea if I would ever see them again, in particular AJ and Howie, which was hard to swallow. However, I wanted them safe. I think the Boys did well with staying in touch with fans. They don't owe us anything but felt it important to stay connected. I appreciated that. I was over the moon happy when they began doing virtual events."

Brian and Howie were the first to do something other than going live on social media. In April, the Littrells livestreamed from their back patio, where Baylee put on a small acoustic concert for fans, with Brian joining in.

Howie went in another direction. On May 15, 2020, Howie was joined by Chef Katsuji Tanabe to teach fans how to cook a special fried chicken recipe. Howie sold tickets to the virtual event, which raised funds for the Trotter Project and CORE, two organizations that help those in the service and hospitality industry. Some fans were lucky enough to score Looped virtual calls with Howie. Looped, at the time, was a new platform that helped fans video chat live with their favorite celebrities.

In July, Nick held Looped phone calls to communicate and talk with fans one-on-one, and AJ, the first Backstreet Boy to use Looped, did the same.

In August 2020, the Backstreet Boys announced a partnership with Apple Music. *All I Have To Give Radio* would be a new radio show where the Boys would talk about their past, things going on today, and the future. Plus, they would have the opportunity to talk to fans.

"We have a very, very loyal fan base that we love so much and appreciate, and we just thought that it would be a really cool opportunity to share those stories with our beloved fan base and people who may not necessarily be fans," Nick told *People* on August 18, 2020. "You'll learn a little bit more about us. We just thought it'd be a cool moment to share some insight into the band."

Nick, having been obsessed with video and computer games since he was a child, joined Twitch, a streaming platform, so that he could play video games and virtually talk with fans. Whether it was early mornings before his kids woke up or late, late nights, screaming when his character was killed, Nick was there to entertain. Sometimes his wife Lauren would come in to tell him to keep it down. As a running joke, there was always some kind of "technical difficulty," since Nick was always trying to perfect his stream.

"COVID was hard, but like always, their music saved my sanity during the lockdown. Although I was still working as I am a healthcare worker, their songs were and are my saving grace," longtime Backstreet Boys fan Jhie Grisola from Ontario, Canada, said. "Nick going live on Instagram was fun, and also AJ's TikTok videos were fun."

"I was glad that the Boys, Nick especially in my case, made so many efforts to keep in touch with all of us all over the world," Barbara added. "What made it bearable was definitely the love I felt even during those hard times. We were living the same struggle together. As much as I missed them, they missed us. So we shared that experience together as well."

During the COVID-19 pandemic, AJ McLean started a business—Ava Dean Beauty. The beauty line, which started out with four different nail polishes, including one clear polish and three named after his wife Rochelle and daughters Ava and Lyric, is vegan and cruelty-free. The nail polishes now come in a variety of colors, featuring special sets for Nick's children, AJ's grandmother, and even a limited-edition set based on the Backstreet Boys themselves.

FRIENDLY COMPETITION

In September, it was announced that AJ McLean would be joining the twenty-ninth season of *Dancing with the Stars*. AJ was partnered with Cheryl Burke, who had previously won season two of the show with 98 Degrees' Drew Lachey and season three with former Dallas Cowboy Emmit Smith. This season would be a little different since they had to have strict health protocols due to COVID-19.

AJ started out strong in the competition, becoming one of the early favorites to win. While he never scored perfectly, during week six, he and Cheryl performed the Samba to "Mi Gente" and received all nines.

However, in week nine, AJ and Cheryl were eliminated, coming in seventh in the competition.

"It still sucks, it's a major bummer, but there's also kind of a sense of relief and calmness as well, because life goes on," AJ told *Entertainment Tonight* after the elimination on November 9, 2020. "I've always been one to bow out from whatever the situation is with ease and grace and with a lot of gratitude. Honest to God, I've

LEFT: Our friend the Crocodile and host Nick Cannon in the "Six More Masks" episode of *The Masked Singer*, September 30, 2020.

made a lot of great friends here, both on the stage and off the stage."

During the competition, AJ, Cheryl, and Rene Elizondo, Jr. (AJ's sponsor and one of his best friends, who also directed the Backstreet Boys' "Chances" music video) began a podcast called *Pretty Messed Up* for iHeartRadio, which was recorded from their homes, safely socially distanced.

Around the same time, Fox's *The Masked Singer* came back with its fourth season. On the second episode of the season, a pink crocodile in a sparkly outfit sang "It's My Life" by Bon Jovi, and Backstreet Boys fans began talking online. Could that be Nick Carter? It sounded like Nick Carter on his very first solo album, *Now or Never*, a phrase that also happened to be included in the lyrics of "It's My Life." It was a fifty-fifty split in the fandom on if that was really Nick or not. Because of how the show is structured, the Crocodile didn't perform for another two weeks, but when he did, he returned with a sultry version of Britney Spears' *Toxic*.

By this point, fans knew it was Nick Carter, thanks to some of the clues in the clue package before the pink Crocodile's performance of the Britney hit. They knew he'd had a toxic childhood and were also familiar with a story that he told in his book about winning a talent competition and giving his father the prize money.

When the Crocodile returned a few weeks later, he stole the show with renditions of Leona Lewis's "Bleeding Love" and Aerosmith's "I Don't Want To Miss A Thing," which was dedicated to his "crocklings" (children). He was up against the Seahorse (Tori Kelly) to make it into the finale, and won. During a special Christmas episode, the Crocodile performed "Silent Night."

In the finale, the Crocodile was up against the Mushroom, who ended up being Aloe Blacc, and the Sun, better known as LeAnn Rimes. He performed "Open Arms" by Journey, which has long been known as one of Nick's all-time favorite songs; he would perform it as a solo during Backstreet Boys shows on early tours. LeAnn ended up winning, and the Crocodile was finally revealed to be Nick, coming in third behind Aloe.

"'The Masked Singer' definitely inspired me to kind of put a little bit of trust into who I am as an entertainer and as a solo artist," Nick told *Entertainment Weekly* at the end of the season. "Of course, I love being a part of the Backstreet Boys and love being the little brother in the group. But it was uncomfortable to be kind of outside the safety net of my group, as far as just being exposed as a solo artist and just from my voice."

ANOTHER YEAR OF COVID-19

With a new year beginning, the world thought COVID might become a thing of the past, but no such luck in 2021. Backstreet Boys fans got their "hit" of their favorite guys when Nick Carter would go live on Instagram or Twitch to make breakfast for his kids. He became known as either "Pancake Daddy" or "Waffle Daddy." Nick and Kevin even did an Instagram live when both of their favorite teams—the Tampa Bay Buccaneers and the Kansas City Chiefs, respectively—played against one another in the 2021 Super Bowl. AJ continued with his *Pretty Messed Up* podcast and did Looped calls.

"Because the DNA World Tour was actively going on and had to be postponed

ABOVE: Nick streams live on Twitch from his home during the COVID-19 pandemic and plays video games with fans.

OPPOSITE: AJ shows off his moves on *Dancing with the Stars* in 2020.

because of COVID, I think the fandom felt the absence a bit more," Danielle Spurge said. "Considering no one knew what to expect or how long postponements would last, I think the Boys did a good job managing expectations and giving fans something to enjoy in the meantime. I loved the radio show series they did with Apple Radio and thought it was so genuine and fun."

"We wanted to personally let you guys know that our 2021 DNA World Tour has been rescheduled until 2022," AJ said in the video as he sat next to the other guys. Australia and New Zealand shows were also pushed back to 2023.

But the real question was, why were all five of the Backstreet Boys together?

BELOW: AJ performs during An Evening to Save Lives: Music For Life at the Westgate Las Vegas Resort & Casino on June 5, 2021.

For the first time in thirty years, the Boys had finally decided to sit down and record a Christmas album. While they had two previous Christmas singles, "Christmas Time" (1997) and "It's Christmas Time Again" (2012), they had never done a full album. With the COVID-19 pandemic putting a stop to touring yet again, they figured it was time.

On March 8, 2021, production on the Christmas album began.

"We had always talked about doing a full-length Christmas album because we all love Christmas music, but just the way our tour cycles and album cycles work—we just never had the time to get it done," Kevin told Billboard's Pop Shop Podcast. "So, quarantine and COVID was a perfect opportunity to have some downtime and make some decisions."

With vaccines becoming available, a little bit of hope began to shine throughout the world—and the Backstreet Boys fandom—that life was going to get back to normal.

On July 12, 2021, the Backstreet Boys really surprised fans—with a Las Vegas Christmas residency! The twelve shows, called A Very Backstreet Christmas Party, would be at their previous Vegas home, Zappos Theater at the Planet Hollywood Resort & Casino, and would run through November and December.

"While the army's been nestled all snug in their beds, and visions of BSB danced through their heads . . . We've planned, and we schemed such a glorious show . . . It's time that we told you! We just want you to know . . . " the Backstreet Boys tweeted, letting their fans in on their holiday surprise.

ABOVE: (L to R) Nick Carter, *NSYNC's Joey Fatone, AJ McLean, and Wanya Morris of Boyz II Men perform the After Party at the Venetian in Las Vegas on August 19, 2021.

Fans began planning trips to Las Vegas for the holidays, especially those in other countries who hoped their travel restrictions would be listed. But fans had a reason to come to Las Vegas earlier. AJ and Nick teamed up with Joey Fatone from *NSYNC and Wanya Morris from Boyz II Men for the After Party, to perform a set of shows in August 2021.

In September, though, the inevitable happened—the Las Vegas residency was canceled, and the Christmas album was pushed back to 2022.

"The past six months, we have been hard at work on our next creative endeavor, a BSB Christmas album. We are so excited and proud of what we have and the way it's all coming together. We feel that this is one of our best creations yet and that this creation deserves the best possible scenario and set up for success," a letter to fans on social media said on September 10, 2022. "With the current state of the world still limiting our travel and causing small things in these processes to take much longer, we have decided to wait until 2022 to release our Christmas album and subsequently will be canceling our limited Las Vegas run of Christmas shows."

The Backstreet Boys weren't the only entertainers who were still canceling shows that had been planned for 2021. Garth Brooks, Florida Georgia Line, BTS, Nine Inch Nails, and more had canceled due to COVID-19 numbers beginning to surge once again.

"During COVID, I never realized how much seeing the Boys in person/concert helped with my anxiety and depression until I went two years without it," Brandy Oakes of Las Vegas, NV, said when thinking about missing the group during the pandemic.

She wasn't alone.

13

I WANT IT THAT WAY

"The last time the Backstreet Boys were in Massachusetts was August 2019 at TD Garden in Boston, and fans were obviously anxious awaiting their return at Xfinity. They did not disappoint. The band came ready to rock and bring back the childhood memories of many in the audience who have been following them for over thirty years."

—Courtney Liston ★ *Sun Chronicle*, July 21, 2022

Entertainment giants: The Boys on screen at the TUI Arena in Hanover, Germany, during the DNA World Tour in May 2019.

BACKSTREET'S BACK (AND SO IS THE WORLD)

As the new year ran into 2022, the world began opening up a little. The US Centers for Disease Control shortened the COVID-19 isolation period to five days, and countries around the world slowly began lifting travel restrictions.

Life was getting back to just a little normalcy, Backstreet Boys fans included.

To kick off the 2022 DNA World Tour, the Backstreet Boys announced four shows in Las Vegas at the Colosseum at Caesars Palace on April 8, 9, 15, and 16, 2022.

"We are extremely excited to get back to work, to get back to entertaining people again," Nick told *People* on an Instagram Live on February 23, 2022. "It's been two years since we stopped our DNA World Tour. We had to stop right in the middle. Vegas will be a celebration kick-off that the DNA World Tour is starting again."

BELOW: The Backstreet Boys perform at their 2022 DNA World Tour stop in Atlanta, Georgia, on June 28, 2022.

When rehearsals began in March, with photos and videos showing up on social media, fans knew it was really happening. For the first time, they could shout "BACKSTREET'S BACK" without the eye roll reserved for lazy headlines about the Boys' "return."

"This is a jam-packed, explosive performance," Nick told the *Today Show* in April 2022. "I think it's the best thing that we've done in years since the late '90s and early 2000s, where we had these really incredible shows with dancing and production."

"We've been at choppin' at the bit. We've been sittin' at home, eatin' waiting to go back out," Kevin joked to Kelly Clarkson that same month during the group's appearance on her talk show. "This show is a great example of our musical legacy. We have all the hits that the fans know and love. We have some new music. Then some gems that were on the albums that are our favorites."

While on *The Kelly Clarkson Show*, the group announced a few more cities were being added to the 2022 DNA World Tour. Since the show only airs in the US, it was announced online that they would also be heading back to Europe in October and November. Due to an overwhelming response in Europe and sold-out shows in Spain, Germany, Italy, Switzerland, and the United Kingdom, more dates for several cities were added.

On April 8, 2022, the Backstreet Boys took the stage for the first time in just over two years. Many fans had seen the show in 2019, but it didn't matter. After the past two years, they could never see it enough.

"We're so blessed to be here with you tonight," Kevin told the crowd, almost tearing up. "It's been two long, hard years. We've all been through a lot." Kevin, the most emotional Backstreet Boy, had a reason to get choked up, especially when they performed "Show Me the Meaning (Of Being Lonely)." He'd lost his mother, Ann, in January.

ABOVE: AJ performs at the 2022 DNA World Tour stop in Atlanta, Georgia, on June 28, 2022.

The next night was another emotional evening as Nick's two-year-old daughter, Saoirse, attended her first Backstreet Boys concert. His son, Odin, had previously attended the Larger Than Life residency and the DNA World Tour in 2019. Saoirse clapped and waved, seeing her father on the screens in the auditorium as she stood in her mother Lauren's lap.

"It's hard to describe the feelings you get whenever you are blessed to take that stage," Nick wrote on Twitter the following day. "Last night's show was one of my most memorable because it was my daughter's first show. Watching both my kids' reactions was something I, and hopefully they, will never forget."

The Las Vegas kick-off and return of the DNA World Tour went off without a hitch—and fans were ready for more.

After a show in Mexico in May, the Backstreet Boys' 2022 DNA World Tour fully began on the road on June 4, 2022, in Chula Vista, CA. And nobody was more excited about the tour being back than the guys themselves, hearing fans scream at the shows.

"It is amazing," AJ told the *Irvine Standard* on June 3, 2022. "I often will remove my in-ear monitor to just feel the moment and hear them sing along. I take it in, I take it in with love."

He expressed even more excitement to *People* on June 8, 2022, about hearing the fans sing back to him after two years of no shows or contact with fans.

"You can see them singing and screaming, but if you can't hear it and you can't feel it right here [points to heart], then what's the fucking point? To be able to still get that level of love and screams twenty-seven years later, it's pretty freaking unremarkable."

BROTHERHOOD AND FAMILY

With the Backstreet Boys back on stage, fans could sense a difference in the guys. They were more playful. It seemed like the tour was more than just a job—but that's because it was. They are brothers, a family. You could see them being playful online while one of the other guys was singing. Nick would constantly pick at Howie while

one of the other guys was singing, or Howie and Kevin would play with Nick when he sat down to do yoga before performing "As Long As You Love Me."

"The five of us are the tightest we've ever been," AJ told *USA Today* on July 19, 2022. "We always talk things out. We'll use constructive criticism and not call anybody out. We talk about it like family because we are. We're all alphas, but at the same time, we're seasoned (pros)."

Brian expressed the same sentiment in a separate interview.

"Today, I could call any of the guys at three, four in the morning and talk through something, and that wasn't the case twenty, thirty years ago," Brian told the *Times Union* on July 20, 2022. "We're emotionally and physically closer now. With success, there can be lots of problems. People split up and do their own thing. This is something uncommon, for a group like ours to stick together for this long. We were kids when we started; now we're all fathers and husbands," he said. "The dynamic now is as close as it's ever been in the past thirty years. People might say, 'Oh, he's lying,' but it's the honest-to-God truth."

The sense of family is something that a lot of fans hold onto, especially now that many have married and/or started families of their own. And those families, especially second-generation Backstreet Boys fans, make going to concerts or watching television experiences that much better.

"Being a mom, it gives me so much joy when I see younger generations enjoying the Boys as much as I did when I was younger," Las Vegas Backstreet Boys fan Brandy Oakes said. "I love that the

BACKSTREET ARMY, ASSEMBLE!

I was introduced to the Boys in the summer of 1996 when we had family visiting from Germany. My cousin told me I had to listen to this album, and she told me confidently I would like them. She was wrong—I didn't like them, I loved them!

My life changed for the better that day as I had come to love music in a way I had never before! It would be the start of my twenty-six-year-and-counting relationship with five complete strangers.

In 2020, in the middle of a global pandemic, my life was changed forever: I was diagnosed with breast cancer at 34. I wasn't allowed to have a support person to come with me to my chemotherapy rounds or radiation treatments. I did, however, have five familiar, safe, and comforting voices to accompany me during chemo and radiation.

Kevin, Howie, AJ, Brian, and Nick, you will never know what security, comfort, and calm you provided to me during the most isolating and horrifying time in my life. With you guys in my ears, I felt like I was getting a hug from not only you but from everyone who couldn't physically be with me. Thank you.

SETA GHARADAGHIAN ★ PHILADELPHIA, PA
KEEPING THE BACKSTREET
PRIDE ALIVE SINCE '96

LEFT: Seta Gharadaghian poses in a handmade T-shirt celebrating Kevin's return.
RIGHT: Nick, Seta's favorite Backstreet Boy, showing the love.

Boys' newer music is still keeping up with today's music trends, but without the use of profanity that so much of the music kids hear today has. It's a good feeling when my kids can enjoy and relate to music without me worrying that they're hearing inappropriate words in their music."

That family feeling came to fruition on June 7, 2022, at the sold-out Hollywood Bowl show in Los Angeles. During the Backstreet Boys' performance of "No Place," which features their families in the music video, their children came out to join them on stage. Nick's two older children, Odin and Saoirse (his youngest, Pearl, was a little too young), Howie's sons Holden and James, Kevin's sons Max and Mason, and AJ's daughters Ava and Lyric, joined the Boys on stage. Brian's son Baylee, an up-and-coming country singer, had a performance in Nashville and was unable to make it.

The children either sported black silk DNA World Tour jackets or retro Backstreet Boys T-shirts. Mason and James were two of the biggest hams on stage, complete with boy band hand moves while singing every single lyric of the song. Lyric and Saoirse, the two youngest Backstreet girls on stage, also sang into their fathers' microphones.

BELOW: The Backstreet Boys are on the marquee at the Hollywood Bowl on May 30, 2022, in Los Angeles.

A VERY BACKSTREET *CHRISTMAS . . .* FINALLY!

In mid-June 2022, at the Backstreet Boys' stop in Rogers, Arkansas, fans who were in their seats early got a little surprise. On the huge screens, fans saw Brian begin to introduce something, and suddenly there were visions of the Boys in Christmas gear, opening presents. "Last Christmas" by WHAM! began playing, but it wasn't George Michael singing—it was the Backstreet Boys.

Suddenly an album cover showing the Backstreet Boys holding a Christmas tree with the words "A Very Backstreet Christmas" above them appeared on the screen with a QR code and link for fans to pre-order. Word immediately began spreading online, though some fans didn't know if it was true or not. But it was very real: there were various versions of the album to order—CD, normal vinyl, an exclusive red vinyl with an autographed cover. The autographed version sold out before morning.

While the videos continued to play at tour stops throughout June and the beginning of July, the official announcement was not made until July 7, 2022.

"We've been wanting to do a Christmas album for nearly thirty years now, and we're excited that it's finally happening," Howie said in a press release on the Boys' official site. "We had such a fun experience putting our BSB twist on some of our favorite Christmas classics and can't wait to be a part of our fans' holiday season."

The album, scheduled for release on October 14, just in time for a little holiday cheer during the spooky season, featured the classics, "White Christmas," "The Christmas Song," "Winter Wonderland," and "Have Yourself a Merry Little Christmas," "Last Christmas," "O Holy Night," "This Christmas," "Same Old Lang Syne," "Silent Night," and "I'll Be Home For Christmas." The album included three original Backstreet Boys Christmas songs: "Christmas in New York," "Together," and "Happy Days."

"We've had a couple Christmas songs, but not this kind of body of work," Nick told ABC Audio on July 8, 2022. "We're excited for people . . . to hear it for the first time. I think that people are going to be really impressed."

TORONTO AND DRIZZY

After the tour ventured through the group's home state of Florida, Georgia, and North Carolina, the Backstreet Boys made their way to Toronto for two sold-out shows. On the second night of the show, there was a sixth honorary member of the group on stage—Drake.

According to the Boys, Drake and Kevin were dining at the same Toronto restaurant when Drake approached Kevin to tell him how the Boys impacted his life.

"At thirteen years old, I had a bar mitzvah, and at my bar mitzvah, for the first time in my life, this girl I was in love with

BELOW: Rapper Drake joins the Backstreet Boys onstage on July 2, 2022, in Toronto, Canada.

came up to me while one of the greatest songs in the world was playing, and she asked me if I would dance with her," Drake said, according to a video from the event posted by the boy band podcast *Boy Band Break*. "It was the first time I ever felt acknowledged, and it was the first time I ever felt like, you know, I had a shot at being cool. If she can see me now, you know what I'm talking about?"

Drake went on to call "I Want It That Way" one of the greatest songs in music history while on stage before the band began singing, with Drake joining in on the chorus, getting the crowd into it more than they already were.

Cinzia Di Franco of Ontario, Canada, a co-host of *Boy Band Break*, was there to see the moment in person.

"We were shocked," Cinzia said. "It was awesome to be so close for such an iconic moment."

During the performance, when it came time for Howie to sing his solo, he integrated Drake's own hit, "Hold On, We're Going Home," into the verses, causing Drake to fanboy even more.

Since the performance in Toronto, Drake has been seen playing "I Want It That Way" at parties on vacation in St. Tropez.

LAST CHRISTMAS

On September 5, 2022, a day before an official announcement was made, fans in North America who signed up for the BSB Insider text messages were sent a message with a photo of Kevin standing in front of a pile of gifts. It included lyrics from the song "Last Christmas" by Wham!: "'Happy Christmas, I wrapped it up and sent it . . .' It's scheduled for delivery tomorrow." Meanwhile, on social media they teased some more about this surprise with "Just a pic from Last Christmas" and a new photo.

Fans outside North America began to notice a new Backstreet song on digital music platforms the next day, shortly after midnight. The song was "Last Christmas," a cover of the Wham! classic and the first song released from *A Very Backstreet Christmas*. The Boys themselves stated they had recorded two music videos, implying that a second single would likely be released.

The Boys officially announced the release of the single via their social media on September 6, 2022. The photo they'd shared the day before on social media was included in the artwork for the single. Fans who pre-saved *A Very Backstreet Christmas* on digital platforms such as Spotify could hear "Last Christmas" instantly. Fans who pre-saved the album and sent a screenshot to the Backstreet Boys' official Twitter would receive "A Very Backstreet Christmas Present."

While a special red vinyl and a normal black vinyl of the album had already been announced, a limited-edition gold vinyl was announced by Spotify for fans who stream the Backstreet Boys' music on their platform. The gold vinyl could only be purchased by fans who received an email from Spotify about it.

"It's a bridge every by-the-book pop act must cross eventually: the Christmas album. And the Backstreet Boys sound like they're all in on their first holiday-themed effort . . .

whether they're embracing vintage doo-wop on 'White Christmas' and 'Winter Wonderland' or going full carol on 'Silent Night,'" the *New York Times* reported on September 8, 2022. "The standout numbers skew more modern: 'Together,' one of three originals, a lite-R&B promise of holiday-season romance."

CELEBRATING THIRTY YEARS

The Backstreet Boys have been teasing special thirtieth anniversary celebrations since COVID, but talk ramped up during the US leg of the 2022 DNA World Tour.

"There are two potentially massive concepts being discussed that would break everybody's brains," McLean told journalist and Backstreet Boys fan Leena Tailor for a *Variety* article in September 2022. "We definitely want to go back to Vegas. Something else I've brought up to the fellas, which they like, is doing a box set for our 30th, but including our 'red' [debut] album, which has never been released in the States."

AJ also mentioned the elusive acoustic album that the group recorded of their previous hits with legendary songwriter Gary Baker, which could be included in a box set. He floated the idea of a ten-part documentary series, too, with each episode highlighting a different album and era.

Nick had another idea—a thirty-song album full of unreleased tracks.

"There's so much stuff in the vault that never got released. It would be great to have it on an album so people don't have to go searching YouTube," Nick told *Variety*.

Several years ago, Brian mentioned doing a multiple-night residency in their hometown of Orlando, FL, where each night would focus on an era of the group's history. Some fans hoped for an anniversary cruise. While it doesn't look like that will happen as of the time of this writing, AJ promises that whatever they do, people will love it.

"We have some interesting tricks up our sleeve," AJ told the UK's Official Charts back in April 2022. "I'll say this: If these things come to light, our fans are literally going to lose their fucking minds."

The Backstreet Boys performing during the first Tecate Emblema 2022 at Autodromo Hermanos Rodriguez in Mexico City, Mexico, on May 13, 2022.

14

NO PLACE

"Jumping from boy band fame to solo stardom is a complex process: once a cog in a well-oiled machine, an artist is being asked to command the spotlight in ways he has never had to before. Many boy band members have attempted the leap, and while some have crashed and burned, others have soared by revealing sides of themselves previously hidden."

—Jason Lipshutz ★ *Billboard*, July 17, 2015

The Boys onstage at *An Evening with the Backstreet Boys* at the Grammy Museum in Los Angeles on April 8, 2019.

LIFE OUTSIDE OF BACKSTREET BOYS

While the Backstreet Boys have been a part of Nick, AJ, Brian, Kevin, and Howie's lives for the past thirty years, they do have lives and careers outside of the group. They are all fathers and husbands and have all taken on their own projects through the years.

NICK
SOLO MUSIC

Nick's solo career outside of the Backstreet Boys began in 2002, when he started working on what would be his first solo album, *Now or Never*. The album was released on October 29, 2002. It peaked at No. 17 on the *Billboard* 200 chart the first week, selling around 70,000 copies. It went on to be certified gold for shipments of 500,000 copies on

December 6, 2002. The album was also certified gold in Canada for shipments of 50,000 and in Japan for shipments of 100,000. It also peaked at No. 4 in Japan. Nick also went on tour in support of the album beginning in February 2003.

It would be nine years before Nick released another solo album, *I'm Taking Off*, in 2011. It was first released in Japan on February 2, 2011, where it would reach No. 8 on the Oricon charts, selling 9,928 copies. The first single, "Just One Kiss," peaked at No. 12 on the Japan Hot 100. In the US, the album was released on May 24, 2011. It never charted, but in Canada, it peaked at No. 12 after its release on August 9, 2011. The Canadian album featured a bonus track that would be released as a single, a song called "Love Can't Wait."

After touring with New Kids on the Block in 2011 and 2012, Nick and New Kids member Jordan Knight worked on an album together titled *Nick & Knight*. The album was released on September 2, 2014, and a tour in support of the album began on September 15 and ran until November 22, 2014.

After placing second on *Dancing with the Stars* in the fall of 2015, Nick released his third solo album, *All American*, on November 25, 2015. He performed the first single, "I Will Wait," on the season finale of the competition. The album featured a guest appearance by Canadian singer Avril Lavigne.

During COVID-19, Nick worked on new solo music and released a song called "'80s Movie" in December 2020 that was very reminiscent of his music from *Now or Never*. A year later, after teasing more solo

BELOW: Nick Carter and Jordan Knight perform as Nick & Knight during their tour stop in Atlanta, Georgia, on October 14, 2014.

The Backstreet Boys were featured in an hour-long episode of the cartoon *Arthur* in 2001. The episode, called "It's Only Rock 'N' Roll," featured the group as rabbits (Brian and Howie) and aardvarks (Nick, AJ, and Kevin), but with their distinctive facial features and hairstyles.

music, he released a song called "Scary Monster," just in time for Halloween. The song came from a small collaboration that Nick did with cryptocurrency company Zombie Inu. In February 2022, Nick released "Easy," a song with country singer Jimmie Allen. The song, which has a mix of country and pop feels, is all about his family.

ACTING AND REALITY SHOWS

Besides solo music, Nick also acted in a few TV shows and films. In 2003, he filmed a movie called *The Hollow*, which was later released during ABC Family's 13 Nights of Halloween in 2004. He also appeared in the MTV movie *Monster Island* as himself. His other acting gigs included *8 Simple Rules*, *American Dreams*, and *90210*. His second major movie was a film called *Kill Speed*. The movie was filmed in 2007, but it was said to have issues with distribution, leading to a 2012 release.

In July 2013, Nick launched a campaign on the crowdfunding website Indiegogo to raise money for his movie *Evil Blessings*. Nick managed to raise $156,214, even though the goal was only $85,000, and planned to use some of his own money to fund the project, as well. Sadly, the movie's director passed away before production started, and the movie was put on hold. Nick instead used the money to film

another movie called *Dead 7*, which ended up being produced by The Asylum—the same company behind *Sharknado*. The movie was filmed in Butte, Montana, in August 2015 and later aired on SyFy on April 1, 2016. The movie featured members from various boy bands, such as Howie and AJ of the Backstreet Boys, Jeff Timmons from

LEFT: Nick looks on at the Nick & Knight tour stop in Atlanta, Georgia, on October 14, 2014.

98 Degrees, the four remaining members of O-Town, and *NSYNC's Joey Fatone and Chris Kirkpatrick.

Nick also filmed two reality shows over the years. In 2006, *House of Carters*

premiered on E! on October 6. Nick and his siblings all lived together in a house in Los Angeles in hopes of reconnecting as a family. The show only lasted one season. The second reality show Nick filmed was *I Heart Nick Carter* in 2014. It showcased Nick and his wife (then fiancée), Lauren, as they planned a wedding around the Backstreet Boys' touring schedule. The show premiered on September 10, 2014, and ran for only eight episodes. The finale, which included footage of their wedding, aired as a one-hour episode on October 29, 2014.

Outside of filming two reality shows about his life, Nick also competed in various shows. Nick was a contestant on *Dancing with the Stars* in the fall of 2015, where his dance partner was Sharna Burgess. He placed second behind Bindi Irwin, daughter of the late Steve Irwin. During the show, Nick and his wife Lauren learned that they were going to be parents of a baby boy.

In the summer of 2017, Nick was an architect on the ABC singing competition show *Boy Band*, in which Nick, Emma Bunton of the Spice Girls, and music producer Timbaland would help guide the contestants throughout the show and find five guys to form a boy band. The show premiered on June 22, 2017, and ran until August 25. It only lasted one season.

As the world was put on hold due to the COVID-19 pandemic in 2020, Nick competed on FOX's singing competition, *The Masked Singer*, where he was dressed as a pink crocodile. Nick placed third that year. Nick has stated that he was offered to be the turtle in 2019 but was too busy at that time to take part in the show.

FAMILY

Nick and his wife, Lauren Kitt, married on April 12, 2014. They have three children:

RIGHT: Nick performs during a Now or Never Tour stop in Valdosta, Georgia, on April 5, 2003.

Seth and Julia McEntire perform to "Everybody" during Seth's wedding reception in 2018.

BACKSTREET ARMY, ASSEMBLE!

My time spent in the fandom started in 1998. I was twenty-nine years old and a mother of two young sons. I loved their sound but based on MTV, their core group was *very* young girls, which I was not. I did sometimes use my young niece or even my own children as an excuse to go to a concert. I mean, the kids did like their music too. My youngest son, Seth, and I even have a couple of special moments we share because of these Backstreet Boys. The first two times I was lucky enough to meet the Boys, Seth was with me, and he met them too. This is something later, thirteen years later, that created a special memory for us. That was the day we planned and executed a pretty cool representation of our relationship through our Backstreet Bys Mother/Son dance at his wedding, where we danced to "The Perfect Fan" and broke into a modification of the "Everybody (Backstreet's Back)" dance. Over twenty-three years have passed with me being the "older" fan. This is not as much of a big deal anymore; we are all just fans. But it did provide memories to cherish.

....

JULIA MCENTIRE ★ LULA, GA
KEEPING THE BACKSTREET PRIDE ALIVE SINCE '98

Odin Reign, born on April 19, 2016; Saoirse Reign, born on October 2, 2019; and Pearl, born on April 21, 2021. They live in Las Vegas, NV.

AJ
SOLO MUSIC

While AJ did solo performances on his own for years (as a British man from Nashville,

TN, named Johnny NoName), it wouldn't be until 2010 when he released his first solo album, *Have It All*. He worked with frequent Backstreet Boys producers and writers Dan Muckala and Kristian Lundin on the album, as well as friend and former *NSYNC member JC Chasez. AJ co-wrote eleven of the twelve tracks, with the one track that he didn't write, "Teenager Wildlife," becoming the first single. The album was released on January 20, 2010, in Europe but was never released in the United States. In 2012, AJ mentioned he had two new songs, "P.L.A.R.S." and "Peach," and that the full album was coming in 2012, but it was never released.

In 2015, AJ released a song called "Live Together" that would be on his next solo album. On the 2016 European Backstreet Boys cruise, AJ performed several new songs, such as "She Wants My Sex," "Love This," "Shot," and "Naked," along with "Live Together." He announced that the album, called *Naked*, would be released on September 6, 2016. It was never released.

After the Backstreet Boys found success in country music with their Florida Georgia Line duet, AJ dipped his toe into Nashville and decided to make a country album. His first country single, "Back Porch Bottle Service," was released on June 4, 2018, during CMA Fan Fest in Nashville. He released three more singles, "Night Visions," "Boy and a Man," and "Give You Away," before finally deciding to go back to his roots.

In 2020, during COVID-19, AJ released a cover of Rihanna's "Love on the Brain," which got a lot of attention from the media and great reviews. In 2021, he relaunched his solo career with "Love Song Love," a song that showed his support for the LGBTQIA+ community; he even dressed in drag in the music video. Another new solo song, "Smoke," was released on July 15, 2022, and is to be released on his next album, *Sex and Bodies*.

ACTING AND REALITY SHOWS

In 2015, AJ appeared in *Dead 7*, the movie that Nick wrote, directed, and starred in. In 2016, AJ was the voice of Kuchimba in an episode of Disney's *The Lion Guard* and voiced Lucy the Fairy in an episode of *The Bravest Knight*. In early 2022, AJ filmed the second season of *Fashion Hero* in South Africa as the host.

In 2020, during the pandemic, AJ was a contestant on the twenty-ninth season of *Dancing with the Stars.* His partner, Cheryl Burke, was a two-time winner, but the couple was eliminated eighth in the competition.

FAMILY

AJ married makeup artist Rochelle on December 17, 2011, and they have two daughters: Ava Jaymes McLean was born on November 27, 2012, and Lyric Dean was born on March 19, 2017. They reside in Los Angeles.

KEVIN
SOLO MUSIC

While Kevin has not released a solo album, he did compose the soundtrack for the 2003 animated movie *The Spirit Bear*.

It was rumored in 2012 that Kevin was working on a solo album. On the 2013

Backstreet Boys cruise, Kevin performed a small solo concert called "Cover Story," which was rumored to be a solo album he was working on of cover songs, and then released one song, a cover of Billy Joel's "She's Got a Way," on YouTube. But nothing else has been said about the album. Fans are still asking about it ten years later.

ACTING

Besides Nick, Kevin has the most acting experience in the group. During the group's break in 2003, Kevin starred as Billy Flynn in *Chicago* on Broadway. After leaving the group in 2006, he returned to *Chicago*,

ABOVE: Kevin onstage at the British Summer Time Festival at Hyde Park in London, United Kingdom, in July 2014.

including performing in the show in Japan in 2007.

He starred in a Christian drama, *Love Takes Wing*, that premiered on the Hallmark Channel on April 4, 2009. He also worked on small, independent films such as *The Bloody Indulgent*, a vampire musical, and the risqué *The Casserole Club*. He won an Independent Vision Award for Best Actor for *The Casserole Club*.

In 2016, *If I Could Tell You*, a short movie Kevin starred in about infertility, was released.

FAMILY

Kevin married longtime girlfriend Kristin in June 2000, and they have two sons together. Mason Frey was born on July 3, 2007, while Maxwell Haze was born on July 10, 2013. They live in Los Angeles.

BRIAN
SOLO MUSIC

Brian signed a solo album deal with Reunion Records in 2004 and released his first album, *Welcome Home*, in 2006. The Christian pop album debuted at No. 3 on the Christian album charts, No. 74 on the Billboard 200 chart, and No. 19 on the Japanese Albums chart.

He released four singles from the album. The first, "Welcome Home (You)," reached No. 1 on Reach FM's Top 40 chart and the R&R Christian Inspirational Chart.

Brian's son, Baylee, released a solo album, *770-Country*, on Brian and Leighanne's personal record label. Brian appears on the song "Come Kiss Me."

It stayed there for three weeks. It also went to No. 2 on the US Christian Charts. Two other singles, "Wish" and "Over My Head," were also released. Another single, "In Christ Alone," went to No. 1 on the Christian charts.

Brian won a Dove Award for Inspirational Recorded Song of the Year in 2006 for "In Christ Alone." He won the same award again for "By His Wounds," off his new album, *Glory Revealed*, in 2008 and also won Special Event Album of the Year for *Glory Revealed*. In 2010, he won another Special Event Album of the Year for *Glory Revealed II*.

FAMILY

While he has not released another solo album, he has released Christmas songs on iTunes that feature his wife, Leighanne, who he married in September 2000, and son, Baylee, who was born November 26, 2002.

The Littrells live in Atlanta, GA.

HOWIE
SOLO MUSIC

Howie began working on a solo album in 2006 that would feature both English and Spanish music but eventually changed his mind and released a full English album. His first album, *Back to Me*, was released on November 15, 2011. The album peaked at No. 56 on the Japanese Albums charts. His first single, "100," was a success in Japan but didn't chart in the United States. He released

OPPOSITE: Brian during Brian Littrell in Concert at Studio Coast in Tokyo, Japan, in February 2006.

Amber and her son goofing off with BSB during a stop on the 2022 DNA World Tour, after her son showed them the onesie they all signed for him before he was born.

BACKSTREET ARMY, ASSEMBLE!

Like many, I have had my share of challenges. I found the Backstreet Boys during a time when I felt alone, with no sense of belonging. When I began following BSB, I connected with others who had similar interests. Since then, I have remained friends with many that I met as a kid, with BSB being one of our shared connections. BSB and its fandom have actually helped me find a place where I belong, where I feel not only accepted, but loved, and can finally be myself and feel safe. These relationships have grown well beyond BSB and fulfill me to this day. Now, as a mother of two, I can introduce my children to something that continues to bring me pleasure. My son attended his first concert, BSB, of course, and it was the most amazing experience to see his delight in their phenomenal show. He was thrilled to sing along to songs that he had been hearing since before he was born. To share that experience with him, not only to see how giddy he was but to feel that connection to him with this shared interest, is something I will take with me for a lifetime.

AMBER W. ★ CENTRAL COAST, CA
KEEPING THE BACKSTREET PRIDE ALIVE SINCE '97

LEFT: Howie and then-girlfriend Leigh Bonielo in 2003.

two more solo singles, "Lie to Me" and "Going Going Gone."

In 2019, Howie released *Which One Am I?*, a children's and family-friendly album.

ACTING AND REALITY SHOWS

In 2015, Howie appeared in *Dead 7*, the movie that Nick wrote, directed, and starred in, and in 2017, Howie and his oldest son, James, appeared on USA's *Big Star Little Star*.

In the winter of 2020, before COVID-19 hit, Howie starred in a play called *Howie D: Back in the Day* that took place at the Rose Theatre in Omaha, NE. The show ran from January 31, 2020, to February 16, 2020, and featured songs from his latest children's album.

In 2021, Howie appeared on TLC's *Long Island Medium: There in Spirit* to connect with his late father and sister. The following year, Howie was a competitor on FOX's *Dirty Dancing*, where celebrities traveled to the location where the movie was filmed and competed in dance competitions.

FAMILY

Howie married longtime girlfriend Leigh in Orlando, FL, on December 8, 2007. The two met when Leigh worked on the Backstreet Boys' website during the *Black & Blue* tour. Their first son, James Hoke Dorough, was born on May 6, 2009. Holden John Dorough was born on February 16, 2013.

15

SOLDIER

....

"Together, Juliana and I ventured into a small subject of the online fan community that, in addition to broadcasting adoration, wrote original jokes and commentary about the packaged persona each member embodied. We launched our BSB humor site on January 1, 2000. By creating the site, Juliana and I immediately became part of something. To me, this period of time felt like the Wild West era of the internet. I, a teen girl, could saunter into a chat room (the online equivalent of a saloon) and announce my presence by slapping my hand on the bar (or by putting some HTML code into a file). I could declare that I belonged, and then, I . . . just did."

—Dena Ogden ★ *The Atlantic*, May 18, 2019

The Boys perform during the DNA World Tour at the iTHINK Financial Amphitheatre on June 22, 2022 in West Palm Beach, Florida.

ROLLERCOASTER OF EMOTIONS

Being a Backstreet Boys fan has never been easy. Whether you were a middle school student in the late '90s who had other students teasing you or you were a middle-aged mother in the early 2000s who loved the band but didn't announce it to the world. Being a Backstreet Boys fan meant growing a thick skin because someone would undoubtedly ridicule you for it. It has been that way for thirty years.

"I would compare being a BSB fan to riding a roller coaster," Medina Goudelock said. "It's the thrill of knowing that what is in front of you will be an amazing ride. It's going to have twists and turns, ups and downs. You're going to feel a huge rush of adrenalin that takes your breath away. When the ride is over, you'll come away with butterflies in your stomach, a crazy smile on your face, and the want for more."

Canadian fan Jhie Grisola agreed. "Being a BSB fan is like going on a rollercoaster ride, because sometimes you're up, happy with the new stuff they release," she said. "Other times, you're down because they take their sweet 'Backstreet Time' to release things we want and have been waiting for."

The Backstreet Boys have always talked about how strong their fans are—which is why we are called the Army. Like the lyric from "Everyone," the Backstreet Boys are "standing strong" because of the fanbase, even though it hasn't always been easy.

In February 2022, Nick attended a convention in Pensacola, FL, where he talked about just that. While he would always get laughed at by other guys his age for being a Backstreet Boy when he was only trying to play basketball while on tour, he knew fans caught the same slack.

"I realized that Backstreet Boys fans also were going through the same thing. We like what we like. We like boy bands. We love what they do, how they make us feel," Nick told the crowd. "I'm proud of our fans for being resilient. I'm proud of our fans for standing up for who they are, what they believe in, what they love. They aren't listening to what the outside world says. That's why we're still here after twenty-eight years. You gotta have faith because being a Backstreet Boys fan isn't easy. Nor is being a Backstreet Boy."

GETTING SOCIAL ON SOCIAL MEDIA

In the late 1990s, finding out what the Backstreet Boys were doing depended on magazines, MTV, chatrooms, newspapers, or their official website. That's no longer the case. Thanks to Facebook, Twitter, TikTok, Instagram, and every other social media platform, we typically know what the guys are doing on a daily basis.

To put it simply, social media has helped humanize the Backstreet Boys for fans.

"Today, we're lucky to hear from the Boys directly on social media, and we no longer need *MTV Cribs* to see glimpses into their home life," Backstreet Boys fan and marketing extraordinaire Brianne Fleming said. "The Backstreet Boys also invites us

What is Backstreet Time? Backstreet Time occurs in one of two ways. Backstreet Time can be when the Backstreet Boys give a date, or range of dates, for a project, such as an album, music video, single, or tour, and it doesn't happen when they say it will. Backstreet Time can also occur in real time, when the group or a group member does not arrive somewhere on time. Used in a sentence: "We have been standing at this deck party for an hour. They are on Backstreet Time."

behind-the-scenes on tour or while making music—and we can engage with them in real time! In a lot of ways, social media feels like an all-access pass!"

Kelly Hanlon of Senoia, GA, agrees. "It's different today because we've all grown up, and we've done it together. I think fans give them a little more space because social media entered the picture, and it's easier to connect that way. That gives them more space and privacy, but they still make every effort to take all the time humanly possible to spend time with fans."

"There's a different level of respect," AJ told *Bustle* in February 2019. He explained that while fans have matured a lot, they do still get mobs of girls chasing after them. "Which is awesome. I mean, what guy wouldn't want a bunch of girls yelling at him? Let's just call a spade a spade. It's fun—still."

"Back in the day, they were totally inaccessible, and you could only find out things from magazines and interviews. Now the Boys will hop on to social media and truly have a chance to connect with their fans. Whether they are wishing someone a happy birthday on Twitter or doing an Instagram live to check in and chat about their day, they are able to interact and get instant feedback," Cinzia said.

Not only is social media the way that we get to hear from the Backstreet Boys themselves, but it's how fans meet one another.

In days of yore (aka twenty or twenty-five years ago), there were things called message boards or forums, plus the Backstreet Boys chatroom on AOL or even on Yahoo, where fans would meet. The Backstreet Boys had their own chatroom during the late '90s and early 2000s on their official website. Sometimes the Boys would pop in to chat as well.

Over the years, there were many fan sites created by fans to share news, photos, media, and more on the group. Many have come and gone, and these days the fan sites are quite limited. Some had their own message boards that brought fans together and were quite popular. But none compared to the message board that was Live Daily. Live Daily was a well-known music website and forum that was owned by Ticketmaster, featuring boards on various artists and topics. This included one for the Backstreet Boys, where many fans met. It was so popular among fans that even Nick himself would browse the forum and go on to mention it in his thank-you notes for the *Never Gone* album.

As a part of the Burger King Backstreet Boys promotion in 2000, Burger King released a VHS called *For the Fans*, which featured behind-the-scenes antics, interviews, and concert footage from the Into the Millennium Tour. While the VHS included only a handful of songs, fans can now see the full footage on YouTube.

Live Daily shut down in 2010, and despite the administrator of the forum creating a new forum After LD, many Backstreet Boys fans moved on. Then social media began to take off, allowing instant communication between friends, fans, and the band. This is where you'll find the Backstreet Army these days.

Social media brings people together who not only love the same group but who possibly have the same favorite member. Then as fans talk about lyrics and dance moves, they also learn about each other's lives—maybe they have the same job or share other similarities. It creates friendships. You can meet your best friend in the Backstreet Boys fandom, on the Official Backstreet Boys Fan Club, on Twitter, or even standing next to them in the pit at a concert.

"My favorite thing about being part of the BSB Army is the friends turned family we all met through the years of being a fan," Jhie explained. "The relationships we formed. We all may not agree all the time, but we also rally for one another when one of us needs us. The connection that we have is a gift."

Twins Kim and Kerry Schussler of Bear, DE, who both share a common love of the Backstreet Boys, agreed—it's the friendships made within the fandom that have meant the most.

"The many years of dedication among so many of us," Kerry said. "The Backstreet Boys have led me to so many incredible friendships over the years, and a lot of these friends I've met through BSB are still my very closest friends currently, who I talk to every single day!"

"I've been friends with Cindy (Allentown, PA) since the NKOTBSB tour and recently met one of my closest friends, April (Vallejo, CA), in Las Vegas at a BSB after party in 2019, and so many other amazing people I'd never have the opportunity to be friends with," Kim said.

"My favorite thing is being able to travel to concerts and events where I see old friends and meet new ones," Medina said. "I especially enjoy doing these things with my bestie, Melly, who I met because of the Backstreet Boys. Eleven years ago, she helped me with a Howie project, and we have been friends ever since."

GROWING UP TOGETHER

"A lot of us in this theater, venue, have been on a ride together for a long time. We want to thank you for being a part of the Backstreet family all this time. Everybody, pretty much, in this room, we grew up together. We've got babies, you've got babies," Kevin told the audience at their July 1, 2022, stop in Toronto. It's something he says, in similar words, throughout the tour.

And he means it.

The Backstreet Boys understand that to their fans, they are family and that fans are

Robin Murray poses with the Backstreet Boys in Las Vegas in 2017.

BACKSTREET ARMY, ASSEMBLE!

I first became a BSB fan in 1997–98, and they have impacted my life in so many ways. I learned photo editing and website building (hello, early HTML and style sheets!) so I could make BSB-related websites, which included hosting friends' fanfic collections. I have used what I learned back then on so many web design projects over the years.

They ignited my love of photography as well. Since I had terrible seats for my earlier concerts, I was determined to get good seats at concerts so I could get my own concert photos that I had seen others share. Some of my favorite shots of mine are from recent BSB shows, including the *In a World Like This* and *DNA* tours.

I have also made so many friends through our mutual love for the guys, including a couple of the longest friendships I've ever had. I've traveled around the country, been to international venues, and done so many other bucket-list-worthy things.

I don't know if I would have experienced or learned these things if I didn't get hooked after hearing "Quit Playing Games" on the radio way back when.

ROBIN MURRAY ★ SPRING, TX
KEEPING THE BACKSTREET PRIDE ALIVE SINCE '97/'98

ABOUT: Kerry Schussler (left photo) and Kim Schussler (right photo) pose with the Backstreet Boys during the 2022 DNA World Tour.

a part of theirs. Some groups do not put those two things together. Some groups do not even think of fans as people, just a number on the album sales chart.

Not the Backstreet Boys.

"Back in the day, Brian used to call fans the CIA," Kelly remembered. "And it wasn't just a few of us. It felt like everyone was able to figure out where the Boys would be and when. One time, we reserved a room at a hotel they were staying at in Albany. After the concert, it began to snow hard. AJ went outside for a cigarette, and my group of friends—who remain some of my closest friends today—ended up having an epic snowball fight with him in the middle of the street. It was exhilarating that despite their being the most famous people in the world, they wanted to connect and have fun with fans."

Stories like that still happen today, whether it's hanging out with Nick or AJ at four in the morning on a Backstreet Boys cruise while eating pizza or running into them in a hotel lobby and being invited to breakfast.

"Now that our fans are older, alcohol is involved," AJ told JoJo Wright on an iHeartRadio Twitter Spaces interview on July 22, 2022. "They're still crazy, still passionate, and we have the best fans in the world, honest to God. If you look out into our crowd right now, I'm seeing kids that are five years old, and I'm seeing people up to eighty. We have such a wide variety of ages in our crowd right now. You're seeing a lot more dudes."

When you say that you are a huge fan of a certain music group, especially a boy band, many think it may be because you think they are cute, or you just like their songs. For a lot of Backstreet Boys fans, it goes much deeper than that. Whether it is the music or meeting the performers themselves, people can get inspired to do things that are good for them that they wouldn't have done if it weren't for the Backstreet Boys.

For Barba Di Mattia from Italy, she learned English because of the Backstreet Boys. They were her "first English teachers."

"I was learning English at school, but everybody who studies a foreign language knows that what you're taught in school has nothing to do with the real spoken language," Barbara said. "So, at first, I was just repeating sounds, and the real lyrics were a mystery to me. But the more you listen, the more you start to pick up expressions and idioms and new words. Thanks to the Boys, I started gradually, then suddenly, to become fluent in English."

She says that it's because of the Backstreet Boys that she has an American accent when she speaks English.

"I used to repeat lyrics in my head, pieces of interviews, and most of my expressions were just me repeating and mimicking what the Boys did or said because I wasn't able to form proper sentences or have a conversation yet," she said. "I became the official song translator of my friend group. Whenever anybody wanted to know what a song was about, they came to me."

For Hilde Schrøder (featured in chapter 2), the Backstreet Boys changed her life in a different way—they gave her something to aspire to. While her weight never stopped her from doing anything before, she set out to have one important goal happen in her next meet and greet.

"My goal was to get a photo with one of them holding me," Hilde said. "I lost the weight for me and my health. But to have that goal helped me over the years. I got my photo."

THE NEXT THIRTY YEARS

Thirty years as a band is a major feat. Thirty years together as a band without breaking up is amazing. Thirty years together as a boy band is a whole different story.

In a 2022 interview with the *Beaver County Times*, Brian was asked if he had pictured still being a Backstreet Boy at his age and still performing. He said he always expected it and anticipated it.

LEFT: The Boys perform at the 2019 iHeartRadio Music Awards at the Microsoft Theater on March 14, 2019, in Los Angeles.

Cindy Arey poses with the Backstreet Boys at a stop on the 2019 DNA World Tour.

BACKSTREET ARMY, ASSEMBLE!

As far back as I can remember, the Backstreet Boys have always been a source of happiness and joy. They feel like home—a place of comfort I can turn to, to escape the realities of life. Their music can make even my worst day seem better. It's rare to find something you connect with so deeply, but I've found that with them, and the feeling is absolutely indescribable. I can always count on them to put a smile on my face, and I will forever be grateful for all the memories they've given me!

CINDY AREY ★ ALLENTOWN, PA
KEEPING THE BACKSTREET PRIDE ALIVE SINCE '97

"And I think we set our goals to be attainable and achievable," Brian said. "But I think our goal always from the very, very beginning was to stick together through the good and bad and just focus on our craft and making good, quality music for a long, long time. And as long as we continue to do that, we can do this for as long as we want. I think that's been the biggest feat from a band like us to be able to achieve."

But what has kept them together for thirty years?

"It's the love of music, the love for each other," Nick told *USA Today* in February 2022. "Every single one of us in this group, we are a family. We see the same goal and dream, and that is to just be entertainers, and honestly, it's the love of our fans. We have the best fans in the world."

For the Backstreet Army, we want nothing more than to see these five guys perform for thirty more years, with canes and in wheelchairs, just like in the video clip they did for the Black & Blue World Tour.

"I absolutely see the Backstreet Boys making more albums and doing more tours," Danielle Spurge said. "The venues, sets, choreography, and length of shows might change, but I do believe they are all performers at heart and wish to continue entertaining for a long time, in whatever capacity they can! They do not appear to be slowing down any time soon."

"I'm hoping they continue touring and creating new music as long as they are happy doing so and making the rest of us and their families happy," Kerry Schussler confessed.

Her sister Kim agreed.

"The only answer I can accept giving is that I hope they're still performing to the best of their ability and, of course, happy and healthy in their personal lives with their families. I'll never be ready for Backstreet Boys to end, no matter how old we all get," Kim Schussler said.

"I see the Boys making more music in the next thirty years, evolving and adjusting to new ways of making music and connecting with fans," Jhie said. "I hope the future holds more Vegas residency dates, new music, and hopefully that a cappella album

we've been hoping and wishing for."

"I don't believe they will ever be done with music," Rachael Jessie said. "I definitely feel like they still have so much more to share. I would love an a cappella album. Maybe even working with their children as Brian has with his son."

The Backstreet Boys have stuck it out for thirty years. When they graced the covers of *Tiger Beat* or *Smash Hits*, nobody thought that would happen. Whatever the future holds for the Backstreet Boys, we know one thing for sure—they will do it together.

And the fans?

The fans aren't going anywhere.

ABOVE: Kelly Hanlon, center, poses with her best friends, Nikki Smith, left, and Courtney Jacobus, right, and the Backstreet Boys during the 2022 DNA World Tour.

INSET: Kelly Hanlon poses with AJ in July 2001 in Boston.

The Boys perform a private
New Year's Eve show at
Caesars Palace Las Vegas
on December 31, 2016.

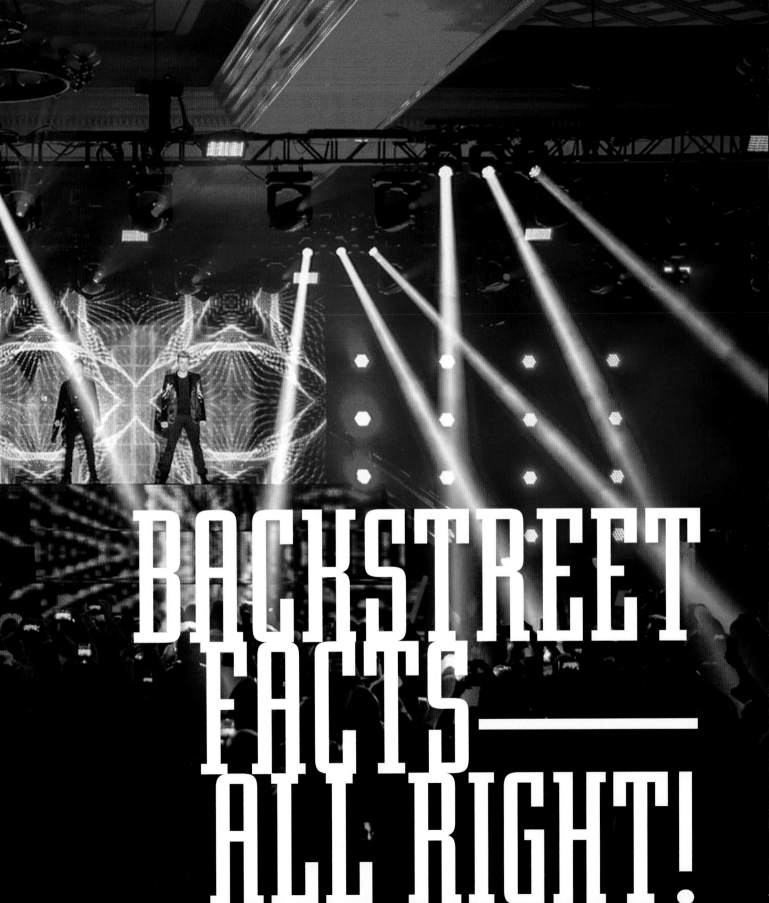

BACKSTREET FACTS—ALL RIGHT!

TIMELINE

1993

April 19, 1993 – Brian Littrell receives a phone call from his cousin Kevin Richardson while sitting in his high school history class in Lexington, KY, about a musical opportunity in Orlando. He flies down the next day.

April 20, 1993 – The Backstreet Boys is formed in Orlando, FL.

May 8, 1993 – The Boys have their first performance at Sea World in Orlando, FL.

1994

1994 – The group signs a record deal with Jive Records.

1995

September 5, 1995 – The group's first single, "We've Got It Goin' On" is released.

1996

May 6, 1996 – The Backstreet Boys' self-titled debut album is released in Europe.

1997

August 11, 1997 – Their second international album, *Backstreet's Back*, is released.

August 12, 1997 – *Backstreet Boys*, their self-titled U.S. debut album, is released.

1998

September 10, 1998 – Backstreet Boys win their first MTV Video Music Award for Best Group Video for "Everybody (Backstreet's Back)." ▼

1999

January 5, 1999 – They receive their first Grammy Award nomination for Best New Artist at the 41st Annual Grammy Awards.

April 12, 1999 – "I Want It That Way" is released.

May 18, 1999 – Their second (US) and third (internationally) album *Millennium* is released. It will go on to sell 1,134,000 copies in its first week of release in the US.

▲
June 2, 1999 – The Into the Millennium Tour kicks off in Belgium.

August 14, 1999 – Tickets for the North American leg of the Into the Millennium Tour go on sale and sell out the same day.

Awards, including Album of the Year for *Millennium*, Albums Artist/Duo/Group of the Year, Albums Artist of the Year, and Artist of the Year.

2000

January 4, 2000 – Backstreet Boys are nominated for four awards at the 42nd Annual Grammy Awards. ▶

November 21, 2000 – The album *Black & Blue* is released worldwide.

2001

January 28, 2001 – They perform the National Anthem at Super Bowl XXXV in Tampa, FL. ▼

July 9, 2001 – The group postpones their Black & Blue World Tour due to AJ McLean going into rehab for drug and alcohol addiction. The tour starts back a few weeks later.

October 23, 2001: *The Hits: Chapter One* is released.

2005

June 14, 2005 – *Never Gone*, their first album in five years, is released.

2006

June 6, 2006 – Kevin Richardson announces his departure from the group.

2007

October 30, 2007 – Their first album as a quartet, *Unbreakable*, is released.

2009

October 6, 2009 – The album *This Is Us* is released.

2010

November 8, 2010 – Backstreet Boys and New Kids on The Block announce a joint tour called NKOTBSB for the

2011

May 25, 2011 – NKOTBSB tour begins in Rosemont, IL.

2012

April 29, 2012 – Backstreet Boys announce Kevin's return to the group during their NKOTBSB show in London, England.

2013

April 20, 2013 – Backstreet Boys celebrate 20 years with a Fan Celebration in Los Angeles.

April 22, 2013 – The group receive a star on the Hollywood Walk of Fame.

June 12, 2013 – The group debuts in their first feature film, the Seth Rogen comedy *This Is the End*, with a cameo at the end.

July 30, 2013 – Their first independent album, *In A World Like This*, is released.

2014

April 13, 2014 – The group wins their first MTV Movie Award for Best Musical Moment for *This Is the End*.

2015

January 30, 2015 – The group's documentary, ▶ *Show 'Em What You're Made Of*, is released.

2016

September 23, 2016 – Backstreet Boys announce their first Las Vegas residency, Larger Than Life.

2017

March 1, 2017 – The Las Vegas residency kicks off. The Boys will perform 80 shows over the next two years. ▼

July 8, 2017 – The Backstreet Boys have their first number one hit on the country charts with "God, Your Mama, and Me," with Florida Georgia Line.

2018

May 18, 2018 – The Boys release the first single from their tenth album, "Don't Go Breaking My Heart."

2019

January 25, 2019 – Their tenth album, *DNA*, is released and debuts at No. 1 on the Billboard 200 chart.

May 11, 2019 – The DNA World Tour kicks off in Lisbon, Portugal.

2022

October 14, 2022 – Their first Christmas album, *A Very Backstreet Christmas*, is released.

2023

April 20, 2023 – The Backstreet Boys celebrate 30 years together.

STREET BOYS

The Backstreet Boys and New Kids On The Block perform together as NKOTBSB in concert at the HP Pavilion in San Jose, California, on July 2, 2011.

GROUP DISCOGRAPHY

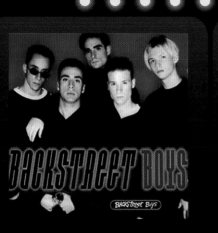

BACKSTREET BOYS (THE RED ALBUM)

Original Release Date: May 6, 1996

Record Label: Jive

SINGLES:

★ "We've Got It Goin' On" (September 5, 1995)

★ "I'll Never Break Your Heart" (December 13, 1995)

★ "Get Down (You're The One For Me)" (April 30, 1996)

★ "Quit Playing Games (With My Heart)" October 14, 1996

★ "Anywhere For You" February 24, 1997

Producers: Denniz PoP, Max Martin, Toni Cottura, Kristian Lundin, Veit Renn, Timmy Allen, Thomas Moore, Bülent Aris

Sales: 10 Million Worldwide

Spotify Streams: 1,369,156,038*

Fact: *Never released in the United States*

BACKSTREET'S BACK

Original Release Date: August 11, 1997
Record Label: Jive

SINGLES:

★ "Everybody (Backstreet's Back)" (June 30, 1997)

★ "As Long As You Love Me" (September 29, 1997)

★ "All I Have To Give" (January 13, 1998)

Producers: Brian Littrell, Kristian Lundin, Max Martin, Timmy Allen, Larry Campbell, P.M. Dawn, Full Force, Robert John "Mutt" Lange, Mookie, Denniz PoP, "Fitz" Gerald Scott

Sales: 1 Million (Canada), 49,334 (Finland), 5 Million (Europe)

Spotify Streams: 374,937,374*

Fact: *This is the first album where one of the Backstreet Boys had a writing credit (Brian for "That's What She Said.")*

BACKSTREET BOYS

Original Release Date: August 12, 1997
Record Label: Jive

SINGLES:

★ "We've Got It Goin' On" (September 5, 1995)

★ "Quit Playing Games (With My Heart)" (June 10, 1997)

★ "As Long As You Love Me" (October 21, 1997)

★ "Everybody (Backstreet's Back)" (June 30, 1997)

★ "I'll Never Break Your Heart (July 14, 1998)

★ "All I Have To Give" (December 8, 1998)

Producers: Denniz PoP, Max Martin, Kristian Lundin, Robert John "Mutt" Lange, Veit Renn, Timmy Allen, Full Force, Aris, Toni Cottura

Sales: Diamond Award – 14 Million (United States)

Spotify Streams: 888,969,351*

Fact: *This album was only released in the United States.*

MILLENNIUM

Original Release Date: May 18, 1999

Record Label: Jive

SINGLES:

★ "I Want It That Way"
(April 12, 1999)

★ "Larger Than Life"
(September 7, 1999)

★ "Show Me The Meaning
Of Being Lonely"
(December 14, 1999)

★ "The One" (May 1, 2000)

Producers: Max Martin, Kristian
Lundin, Rami Yacoub, Timmy Allen,
Robert John "Mutt" Lange, Stephen
Lipson, Eric Foster White, Mattias
Gustafsson, Edwin "Tony" Nicholas

Sales: 24 Million (Worldwide),
15.4 Million (United States)

Spotify Streams: 1,369,156,038*

Fact: *As of 2016,* Millennium *stood
as the fifth best-selling album in
the United States.*

BLACK & BLUE

Original Release Date:
November 21, 2000

Record Label: Jive

SINGLES:

★ "Shape of My Heart"
(October 3, 2000)

★ "The Call" (February 6, 2001)

★ "More Than That" (May 29, 2001)

Producers: Max Martin, Rami Yacoub,
Timmy Allen, Babyface, Larry "Rock"
Campbell, Franciz & LePont, Rodney
Jerkins, David Kreuger, Kristian Lundin,
Per Magnusson

Sales: 15 Million (Worldwide)

Spotify Streams: 395,753,802*

Fact: Black & Blue *is the Backstreet
Boys album that sold the most copies in
one week (1.5 million).*

NEVER GONE

Original Release Date: June 14, 2005

Record Label: Jive

SINGLES:

★ "Incomplete"
(April 1, 2015)

★ "Just Want You To Know"
(October 4, 2005)

★ "Crawling Back To You"
(October 11, 2005)

★ "I Still"
(January 31, 2006)

Producers: Rami, Johan Brorson,
Dr. Luke, John Fields, Billy Mann,
Max Martin, Victoria Wu, Dan Muckala,
Mark Taylor, Christian Nilsson,
John Shanks, Supa'Flyas, Gregg
Wattenberg, Paul Wiltshire

Sales: 3 Million (Worldwide)

Spotify Streams: 158,707,671*

Fact: *The single for "Incomplete" went
gold in the US, selling over 500,000
copies.*

Spotify streaming numbers as of August 2022.

UNBREAKABLE

Original Release Date:
October 30, 2007

Record Label: Jive

SINGLES:

★ "Inconsolable"
(August 27, 2007)

★ "Helpless When She Smiles"
(January 15, 2008)

Producers: JC Chasez, Emanuel Kiriakou, Dan Muckala, David Hodges, Rob Wells, Adam Anders, John Shanks, Billy Mann, Neff-U, Kara DioGuardi, Mitch Allan

Sales: 1.5 Million (Worldwide)

Spotify Streams: 59,833,509*

Fact: *The album opens with a one-minute a cappella version of the chorus of "Unsuspecting Sunday Afternoon."*

THIS IS US

Original Release Date:
October 6, 2009

Record Label: Jive

SINGLES:

★ "Straight Through My Heart"
(August 17, 2009)

★ "Bigger"
(December 14, 2009 – UK,
February 1, 2010 – US)

Producers: Ryan Tedder, Jim Jonsin, T-Pain, RedOne, Emanuel Kiriakou, Brian Kennedy, Printz Board, Soulshock & Karlin, Claude Kelly, Max Martin, Mr. Pyro, Michael Mani, Troy Johnson, Antwoine Collins, Jordan Omley

Sales: 750,000 (Worldwide)

Spotify Streams: 61,080,273*

Fact: *A bonus track in the United Kingdom, "Helpless," featured Pitbull.*

NKOTBSB

Original Release Date: May 24, 2011

Record Label: Legacy, Columbia, Jive

SINGLES:

★ "Don't Turn Out The Lights" (with New Kids on the Block)
(April 5, 2001)

Fact: *The album featured another song, "All In My Head," which was originally recorded for a Backstreet Boys album.*

IN A WORLD LIKE THIS

Original Release Date:
July 30, 2013

Record Label: K-BAHN,
BMG Rights Management

SINGLES:

★ "In A World Like This"
(June 25, 2013)

★ "Show 'Em What You're Made Of"
(November 18, 2013)

Producers: Max Martin, Kristian
Lundin, Martin Terefe, Glen Scott,
Andreas Olsson, Morgan Taylor Reid,
Jordan Omley, Dan Muckala, Justin
Trugman, Jaakko Manninen

Sales: 450,000 (Worldwide)

Spotify Streams: 82,124,109*

Fact: *This is the first Backstreet Boys
album to be released on their own label,
K-BAHN.*

DNA

Original Release Date: January 25,
2019

Record Label: RCA, K-Bahn

SINGLES:

★ "Don't Go Breaking My Heart"
(May 17, 2018)

★ "Chances"
(November 9, 2018)

★ "No Place"
(January 4, 2019)

Producers: Ryan Tedder, The
Stereotypes, Andy Grammer, Stuart
Crichton, Kuk Harrell, Jamie Hartman,
Ryan OG, Lauv, Ben Bram, Elof
Loelv, Jake Troth, The Wild, Mitch
Allan, Ian Kirkpatrick, Zach Skelton,
Steve James, Steven Solomon, Ross
Copperman, Josh Kear

Sales: 303,000 (US physical albums,
as of January 1, 2020)

Spotify Streams: 248,682,471*

Fact: *This is the Backstreet Boys' third
No. 1 album, which means they've had
number-one albums in three decades:
the 1990s, 2000s, and 2010s*

A BACKSTREET CHRISTMAS

★ **Original Release Date:**
October 14, 2022

Producers: Ryan Tedder, The
Stereotypes, Andy Grammer, Stuart
Crichton, Kuk Harrell, Jamie Hartman,
Ryan OG, Lauv, Ben Bram, Elof Loelv,
Jake Troth, The Wild, Mitch Allan, Ian
Kirkpatrick, Zach Skelton, Steve James,
Steven Solomon, Ross Copperman,
Josh Kear

COMPILATION

THE HITS – CHAPTER ONE
Original Release Date:
October 23, 2001
Record Label: Jive
SINGLES:
★ "Drowning"
(October 16, 2001)

Sales: 6 Million (Worldwide)

Fact: *A VHS and DVD were released along with this album, featuring the music videos for each song.*

SOLO DISCOGRAPHIES

NICK CARTER
NOW OR NEVER
Original Release Date: October 29, 2002
Record Label: Jive
SINGLES:
★ "Help Me" (September 3, 2002)
★ "Do I Have To Cry For You" (November 11, 2002)
★ "I Got You" (February 14, 2003)

I'M TAKING OFF
Original Release Date: May 24, 2011
Record Label Kaotic INC, 604, Sony

SINGLES:
★ "Just One Kiss" (January 28, 2011)
★ "I'm Taking Off" (May 31, 2011)
★ "Love Can't Wait" (June 21, 2011)
★ "Burning Up" (January 24, 2012)

NICK & KNIGHT (WITH JORDAN KNIGHT)
Original Release Date:
September 2, 2014
Record Label: Nick & Knight, Mass Appeal, BMG
SINGLES:
★ "Just The Two Of Us" (May 2, 2014)
★ "One More Time" (July 15, 2014)

ALL-AMERICAN
Original Release Date: November 25, 2015
Record Label: Kaotic, Inc.
SINGLES:
★ "I Will Wait" (September 12, 2015)
★ "19 in 99" (February 5, 2016)
OTHER SINGLES:
★ "80s Movie" (2020)
★ "Scary Monster" (2021)
★ "Easy" (with Jimmie Allen) (2022) As Featured Artists
★ "Oh Aaron" by Aaron Carter (2001)
★ "Not Too Young, Not Too Old" by Aaron Carter (2001)
★ "She Wants Me" with Aaron Carter (2003)
★ "Come Together Now" with various artist (2005)
★ "Beautiful Lie" with Jennifer Paige (2009)

HOWIE DOROUGH
BACK TO ME
Original Release Date: November 9, 2011

Label: Avex Group, HowieDoItMusic

SINGLES:
★ "100" (June 3, 2011)

★ "Lie To Me" (October 4, 2011)

★ "Going Going Gone" (February 28, 2012)

WHICH ONE AM I?
Original Release Date: July 12, 2019

Label: HowieDoItMusic

SINGLES:
★ "No Hablo Espanol" (2019)

★ "The Me I'm Meant To Be" (2019)

★ "Monsters In My Head" (2019)

OTHER SINGLES
★ "I'll Be There" with Sara Geronimo

★ "If I Say" with U

AS FEATURED ARTIST:
★ "Show Me What You Got" with Bratz and BoA

★ "It Still Matters" with The Gospellers

★ "New Tomorrow" with A Friend In London

AJ MCLEAN
HAVE IT ALL
Original Release Date: January 20, 2010

Label: Avex

SINGLES:
★ "Teenage Wildlife" (2010)

OTHER SINGLES:
★ "Live Together" (2015)

★ "You" (2015)

★ "Back Porch Bottle Service" (2018)

★ "Night Visions" (2018)

★ "Boy and a Man" (2019)

★ "Give You Away" (2019)

★ "Love On The Brain" (2020)

★ "Love Song Love" (2021)

★ "Smoke" (2022)

AS FEATURED ARTIST:
★ "Clouds" with Redrama (2013)

BRIAN LITTRELL
WELCOME HOME
Original Release Date: May 2, 2006

Label: Reunion, Sony BMG

SINGLES:
★ "In Christ Alone" (February 15, 2005)

★ "Welcome Home (You)" (January 28, 2006)

Label: BriLeigh Records
★ "Baby It's Cold Outside" with Leighanne Littrell (2010)

★ "I'll Be Home For Christmas" (2010)

AS A FEATURED ARTIST:
★ "I Surrender All" (2007)

★ "By His Wounds" with Mac Powell, Mark Hall and Steven Curtis Chapman (2007)

★ "You Alone" (2007)

★ "I'll Fly Away Medley" with Candi Pearson-Shelton, Mac Powell, Shane Evertt, Shane Barnard, Shawn Lewis and Trevor Morgan

★ "How Great" with Mac Powell, Jonathan Shelton, Shane Everett

★ "Come Kiss Me" with Baylee Littrell (2019)

FILMOGRAPHIES

BACKSTREET BOYS

- *Sabrina The Teenage Witch* (1998)
- *Arthur: It's Only Rock N' Roll* (2002)
- *This Is The End* (2013)
- *Show 'Em What You're Made Of* (Documentary) (2015)
- *Undateable* (2016)

NICK CARTER

- *Edward Scissorhands* (1990 – uncredited)
- *American Dreams* (2022)
- *8 Simple Rules* (2003)
- *The Hollow* (2004)
- *Monster Island* (2004)
- *House of Carters* (2006)
- *Kill Speed* (2010)
- *The Pendant* (2010)
- *90210* (2012)
- *I (Heart) Nick Carter* (2014)
- *Dead 7* (2016)

HOWIE DOROUGH

- *Parenthood* (1989)
- *Welcome Freshmen* (1990)
- *Roswell* (2000)
- *Dora The Explorer* (2002–2004)
- *Sabrina The Teenage Witch* (2002)
- *Constellation* (2005)
- *Dead 7* (2016)

BRIAN LITTRELL

- *Olive Juice* (2000)
- *Megalodon* (2002)
- *Pistachio – The Little Boy That Woodn't* (2011)
- *Dynasty* (2021)

AJ MCLEAN

- *Truth or Dare* (1986)
- *Hi Honey, I'm Home!* (1991)
- *Nickelodeon GUTS* (1992)
- *Welcome Freshmen* (1993)
- *Olive Juice* (2000)
- *Static Shock* (2002)
- *Dead 7* (2016)
- *The Lion Guard* (2018)
- *The Bravest Knight* (2019)
- *Days Of Our Lives* (2021)

KEVIN RICHARDSON

- *My Girl* (1991)
- *Love Takes Wing* (2009)
- *The Casserole Club* (2010)
- *The Bloody Indulgent* (2012)
- *If I Could Tell You* (2016)
- *Vampire Burt's Serenade* (2020 – new edit of "The Bloody Indulgent")

- Television
- Film

AWARDS & NOMINATIONS

1995
★ WON

Smash Hits Awards – Best New Tour Act

1996
★ WON

Goldene Kamera (Germany)
 – Best Boyband

MTV European Music Awards –
 MTVSelect "Get Down (You're the
 One For Me)"

Viva Comet Awards – Durchstarter
 (Best Newcomers) and The Shooting
 Star of the Year

1997
★ NOMINATED

Premios Amigos – International:
 Best Group

★ WON

Bravo Otto – Gold Pop Group

MTV European Music Awards – Select
 Award (Viewer's Choice) "As Long
 As You Love Me"

Smash Hits Awards – Best Band On
 Planet, Best International Band, Best
 Album: "Backstreet's Back"

Diamond Award for their debut
 album *Backstreet Boys* selling over
 1,000,000 copies in Canada.

Viva Comet Awards – Durchstarter
 (Best Newcomers), Band of the Year
 (US Choice)

1998
★ NOMINATED

American Music Awards – Best Adult
 Contemporary Artist and Best Group

MTV European Music Awards – Best
 Group and Best Pop Act

MTV Video Music Awards – Best
 Dance Video

★ WON

Billboard Music Awards – Group Album
 of the Year for *Backstreet Boys*

Bravo Otto – Gold Pop Group

Echo Awards – Best International
 Group

MuchMusic Video Awards – Peoples
 Choice Favorite International Group

MTV Video Music Awards – Best
 Group Video "Everybody
 (Backstreet's Back)"

Prix Gemini Awards – Best
 Performance in a Variety Program
 or Series

Smash Hits Poll Winners awards –
 Best Non-British Act

TMF Awards (Netherlands) – Best
 International Album: "Backstreet
 Boys", Best International Single:
 "As Long as You Love Me", and
 Best International Live Act

Viva Comet Awards – Durchstarter
 (Best Newcomers) and Band of
 the Year (US Choice)

World Music Awards – World's Best
 Selling Dance Act

1999
★ NOMINATED

American Music Awards – Favorite
 Adult Contemporary Artist

Grammy Awards – Best New Artist

MTV European Music Awards – Best
 Pop Artist, Best Album (*Millennium*)
 and Best Song ("I Want It
 That Way")

MTV Video Music Awards – Best Group
 Video and Video of the Year

People's Choice Awards – Favorite
 Musical Group or Band

★ WON

American Music Awards – Favorite
 Pop/Rock Band, Duo or Group

Billboard Music Awards – Album of the
 Year for *Millennium*, Albums Artist/
 Duo/Group of the Year, Albums Artist
 of the Year, and Artist of the Year

Blockbuster Entertainment Awards
 – Favorite CD for *Millennium* and
 Favorite Group-Pop

Bravo Otto – Silver Band

Industry's Best Seller Award 99 –
 Record of the Year

International Kids Choice Awards –
 Best Music Group in Latin America
 and Brazil

MTV European Music Awards – Best
 Group

MTV Video Music Awards – Viewer's
 Choice "I Want It That Way"

MuchMusic Video Awards – People's
 Choice Favorite International Group

Nickelodeon Kids Choice Awards
– Favorite Song "Everybody
(Backstreet's Back)"
Pollstar Concert Industry Award –
Most Creative Stage Production
Smash Hits Poll Winners Awards – Best
Band on the Planet Pop,
Best Non-British Band, Best Single
of 1999 "I Want It That Way",
Best Album of 1999 for *Millennium*,
Best Pop Video for "Larger
Than Life"
Teen Choice Awards – Choice Music
Video of the Year "All I Have to Give"
TMF Awards – Best Live International
Act 99
Viva Comet Awards – Zuschauer-
Comet Viva (Viewers' Choice)
World Music Awards – World's Best
Selling Pop Group, World's Best-
Selling R&B Group, and World's
Best Selling Dance Group

2000
★ NOMINATED
American Music Awards – Favorite
Pop/Rock Album (*Millennium*)
Grammy Awards – Best Pop
Performance by a Duo or Group,
Record of the Year, Song of the
Year ("I Want It That Way"), Best
Pop Album, and Album of the Year
(*Millennium*)
MuchMusic Awards – Favorite
International Group

★ WON
American Music Awards – Favorite
Pop/Rock Band, Duo or Group
Bravo Otto – Gold Pop Group
Juno Awards – Best-selling Album
(foreign or domestic): *Millennium*
Latino Nickelodeon Kids Choice
Awards- Best Group, Best song
"Larger Than Life", Favorite Star, and
Best R&B Group

MTV Europe Music Awards
– Best Group
MTV IMMIES (India) – Best Pop, Best CD
Nickelodeon Kids Choice Awards –
Favorite Music Group
People's Choice Awards – Favorite
Musical Group or Band
Teen Choice Awards – Choice Album:
Millennium
TV Hits Awards – Outstanding
Contribution to Pop
Radio Music Awards – Radio Slow
Dance Song Of The Year: "Show Me
the Meaning of Being Lonely"
World Music Awards – World's
Best-selling American Group,
World's Best-selling Pop Group,
World's Best-selling R&B Group,
and World's Best-selling
Dance Artist

2001
★ NOMINATED
Grammy Awards – Best Pop
Performance by a Duo or Group with
Vocal ("Show Me the Meaning of
Being Lonely")
MTV Video Music Awards – Best Pop
Video, Viewer's Choice
Nickelodeon Kid's Choice Awards –
Favorite Singing Group

★ WON
American Music Awards – Favorite
Pop/Rock Band, Duo or Group
MuchMusic Video Awards – People's
Choice Favorite International Group
TMF Awards (Netherlands) – Best
International Pop Group
World Music Awards – World's Best
Selling Pop Group and World's Best
Selling American Group

2002
★ NOMINATED
Grammy Awards – Best Pop
Performance by a Duo or Group with
Vocal ("Shape of My Heart")

★ WON
RIAJ – 7th Japan Gold Disc Award
2002 MTV Asia Awards – Favorite
Video
"The Call"
MTV Video Music Awards Japan
– Best Group

2003
★ WON
MTV TRL Awards – Sneak Attack (for
fake satellite interview in 2001)

2005
★ NOMINATED
MTV Latin American Awards – Favorite
International Artist
Teen Choice Awards – Choice Love
Song: "Incomplete"

★ WON
Bravo Otto – Bronze Pop Group

2006
★ NOMINATED
Nickelodeon Kids Choice Awards –
Favorite Music Group
TRL Awards Italy – Best Group

★ WON
Bravo Otto – Superband Pop 2005
MTV Asia Awards – Favorite Pop Act
The Recording Academy Honors – to
mark their success in the Music
industry so far.

2010
★ WON
Japan Gold Disc Award – International Song of the Year: "Straight Through My Heart"

2011
★ WON
NewNowNext Awards – Best New Indulgence: New Kids On The Block/Backstreet Boys Summer Tour 2011

2013
Star on the Hollywood Walk of Fame

2014
★ NOMINATED
World Music Awards – Best Live Act, Best Album, and Best Group
★ WON
MTV Movie Awards – Best Musical Moment (Performance of "Everybody (Backstreet's Back)" in the movie *This Is The End*)

2017
★ NOMINATED
Teen Choice Awards – Choice Collaboration and Choice Country Song Florida Georgia Line Feat Backstreet Boys "God, Your ; Mama, and Me"
★ WON
Best of Las Vegas – Best New Act/Show for their "Larger Than Life" Las Vegas Residency

2018
★ NOMINATED
Teen Choice Awards – Choice Pop Song for "Don't Go Breaking My Heart"
★ WON
CMT Music Awards – 2018 CMT Performance of the Year for BSB and Florida Georgia Line's performance of "Everybody (Backstreet's Back)" on *CMT Crossroads*
Best of Las Vegas – For their Larger Than Life Residency
Gold – Best Resident Performer/Headliner and Best Production Show
Silver – Best Bachelorette Party

2019
★ NOMINATED
Grammy Awards – Best Pop Duo/Group Performance "Don't Go Breaking My Heart"
MTV Video Music Awards – Best Group
★ WON
BMI Pop Award – Award-winning Song "Don't Go Breaking My Heart"
Vina del Mar International Song Festival – "Gaviota de Plata" (Silver Seagull) and "Gaviota de Oro" (Golden Seagull)

DEDICATION

This book is dedicated to my mama, Cheryl, who passed away while this book was in the design process. She took me to my first boy band concert in fourth grade (NKOTB). She supported my Backstreet Boys love and loved them herself, seeing them a few times.
I love you, Mama.

—Karah-Leigh

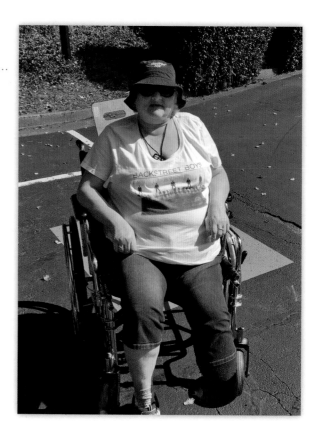

ACKNOWLEDGMENTS

This book would not have been possible without the opportunity from Quarto Publishing. Thank you to Cara, Rage, Katie, and the entire team. We will never be able to thank you enough.

Thank you to our fellow girls at BSBFangirls.com, Melly and Amber, and visitors for putting up with us while we wrote this book.

Thank you to Kat, Eddie, Jen, Justin, Mike, Josh, Keith, and the entire Backstreet Boys crew for always being so great, whether it's cruises, shows, or events in general. You guys are true rockstars.

To all the Backstreet Boys fans, whether we have met, just talked online, or never spoken at all. Deep down, we are a family. We are the Backstreet Army. Thank you for supporting those five guys we love so much.

And to the Backstreet Boys—AJ, Brian, Kevin, Nick, and Howie (yes, we did the Neptunes' rap sequence)—we may tell you, or you may read it online or in this book, but you will never really know what you mean to us, and fans around the world, because you guys mean the world to us. Happy thirtieth anniversary, y'all. Now let's eat cake.

AARON CARTER
1987-2022

On Saturday, November 5, 2022, news broke that Aaron Carter, Nick's younger brother, passed away at his home in California.

Aaron was affectionately known throughout his childhood and career as the Backstreet Boys' little brother. He toured with the group, as well as with *NSYNC, Britney Spears, and more pop superstars, and released his first album, *Aaron Carter*, in 1997. The album featured a song that was co-written by Nick and Brian called "Ain't That Cute." The album went on to sell a million copies, and a star was born.

Aaron would go on to release four more albums, including the multi-platinum *Aaron's Party (Come Get It)*, *Oh Aaron*, and *Another Earthquake*, carving his own path in the entertainment industry.

ABOVE: Brian, Kevin, Nick, AJ, and Howie with Aaron (center) in Hawaii in 1997.

The day after Aaron's death, the Backstreet Boys continued their DNA World Tour in London, where photos of Aaron and Nick filled the screens as they finished singing their single, "No Place," a song about their families.

"Tonight, we've got a little bit of heavy hearts, because we lost one of our family members yesterday and we just wanted to find a moment in our show to recognize him," Kevin told the crowd as they cheered. Nick became upset and his bandmates hugged him, with AJ leading the charge.

"My heart is broken. Even though my brother and I have had a complicated relationship, my love for him has never ever faded. I have always held on to the hope that he would somehow, someday want to walk a healthy path and eventually find the help that he so desperately needed. Sometimes we want to blame someone or something for a loss, but the truth is that addiction and mental illness is the real villain here. I will miss my brother more than anyone will ever know. I love you Chizz. Now you can finally have the peace you could never find here on earth . . . God, please take care of my baby brother." —Nick on Instagram

ABOUT THE AUTHORS

Karah-Leigh Hancock

Karah-Leigh Hancock is a former award-winning journalist and pop culture expert who now works in digital marketing. She has a Bachelor's degree in Mass Media with minors in Creative Writing and Journalism.

She became a Backstreet Boys fan on May 1, 1998, at Grad Nite, when Nick Carter looked down at her and asked if he was sexual while singing "Everybody (Backstreet's Back)." She said yes, and the rest is history.

Karah-Leigh has been featured in various books, articles, shows, and podcasts for her fangirl and pop culture knowvledge. She was crowned the Trivia Queen on the 2018 Backstreet Boys cruise by Nick and is known for her random Backstreet knowledge and archives. While she currently owns BSBFangirls.com with co-writer Emilia, she also has a long history of running fan sites (and even writing fan fiction!). She also has two Backstreet Boys-related tattoos.

In her spare time, Karah-Leigh enjoys writing fiction, designing T-shirts, going to concerts and traveling the world with her best friends Julia, Mara, and Lisa, and seeing her many BSB friends, the Marvel Cinematic Universe, the Atlanta Braves, and binging TV shows.

Twitter: @KarahTheFangirl / @BSBFangirls
Instagram: @KarahLeigh / @BSBFangirls
Online: karahleigh.com / bsbfangirls.com

Emilia Filogamo

Emilia has been a Backstreet Boys fan since early 1998. She was born in Naples, Italy, but currently lives in Pittsburgh, Pennsylvania. In the summer of 2006, she created a fan site about Nick Carter. The website was a hobby and her way of showing support for Nick and the Backstreet Boys. It became a popular website among fans to get news on the group and Nick. During the twelve years that she has owned the fan site, she received an opportunity to work on Nick's official website in June 2012, posting news regarding his career. She currently co-owns BSBFangirls.com, a fan blog for Backstreet Boys news and blogs written by fans. Besides being a Backstreet Boys fan, Emilia loves to read books, write, listen to music, watch movies, and watch soccer.

Twitter: @KaosOnline / @WrittenStars85
Instagram: @kaos_online / @writtenstars85

PHOTO CREDITS

INDEX

Inspiring | Educating | Creating | Entertaining

Brimming with creative inspiration, how-to projects, and useful information to enrich your everyday life, quarto.com is a favorite destination for those pursuing their interests and passions.

Epic Ink titles are also available at discount for retail, wholesale, promotional, and bulk purchase. For details, contact the Special Sales Manager by email at specialsales@quarto.com or by mail at The Quarto Group, Attn: Special Sales Manager, 100 Cummings Center Suite 265D, Beverly, MA 01915 USA.

22 23 24 25 26   5 4 3 2 1

ISBN: 978-0-7603-8224-0

Library of Congress Control Number: 2022945152

Publisher: Rage Kindelsperger
Creative Director: Laura Drew
Managing Editor: Cara Donaldson
Editor: Katie McGuire
Text: Karah-Leigh Hancock and Emilia Filogamo
Cover Design: Scott Richardson
Interior Design: Kegley Design

Printed in China